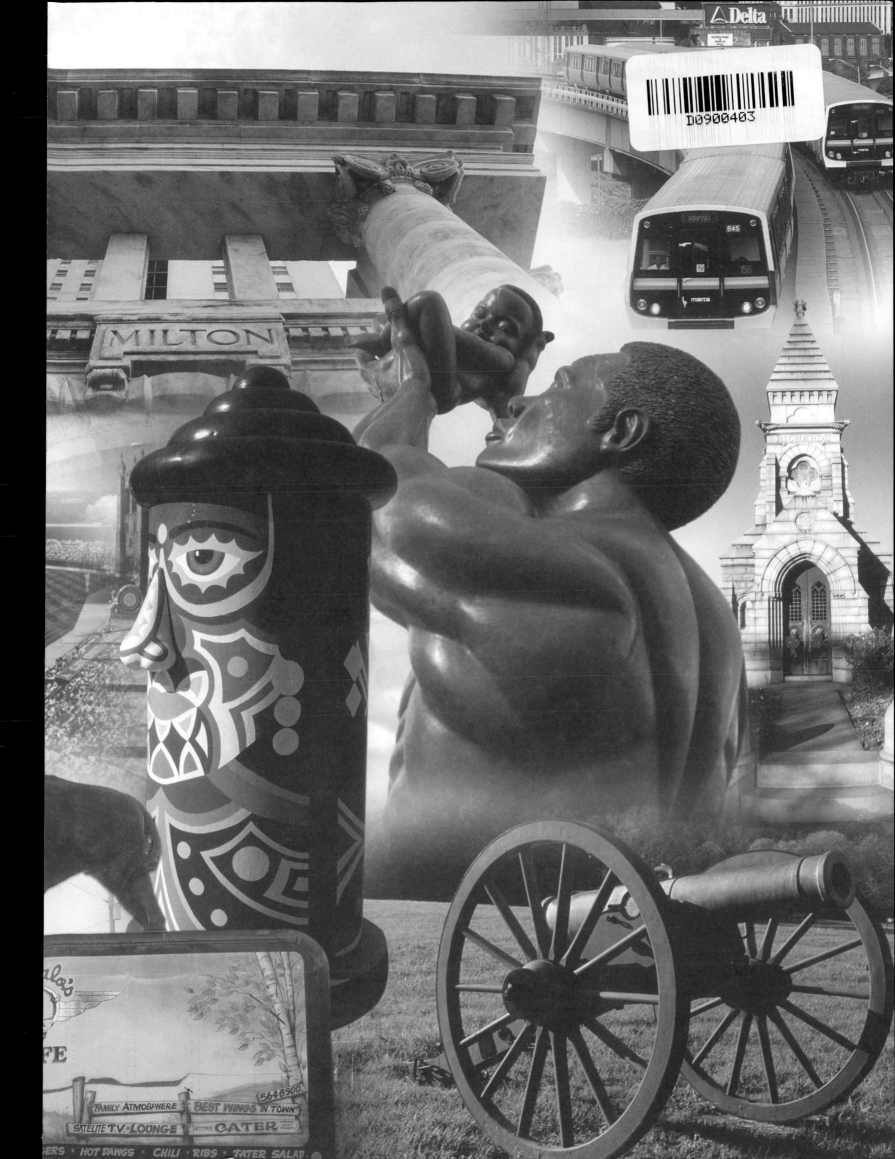

ATLANTA

in focus

Introduction by *Jimmy Carter*

Published by: Imprint Publications, LLC
www.imprintpublications.com
ISBN: 09754154-2-5
Library of Congress Control Number: 2004114777
First Edition
Publisher: *Charles Parks*
Editorial Director: *Lori M. Parks*
Art Director. *Gina Mancini*
Editor-In-Chief: *Betsy Blondin*
Project Manager: *Ron Beers*
Profile Coordinators: *Mary Campbell, Linda Johnson*
Color & Image Artist: *Kristi Campbell*
Administration: *Vicki Verne, Juan Diaz*
Profile Writers: *Karuna Eberl, Allen Gardiner, Jessica Halliday,
Carol Patton, Alexis Pedersen, Ron Raposa, Alli Rainey Wendling*

We must **ADJUST** to changing times
and still hold to **unchanging** **PRINCIPLES**.

Jimmy Carter

TABLE OF CONTENTS

PARTNERS IN ATLANTA

For their significant leadership in the development of this project, the following organizations are recognized. Their contributions make this book a greater success and are appreciated.

THE
CARTER CENTER

Waging Peace. Fighting Disease. Building Hope.

The Coca-Cola Company
Coca-Cola Enterprises Inc.

KING & SPALDING LLP

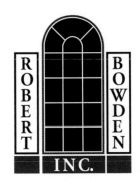

Introduction

By Jimmy Carter

"ATLANTA has vitality and influence and is prospering socially and economically."

Jimmy Carter

When I was growing up on a peanut farm in Plains during the Great Depression, I saw Atlanta as an exciting, mysterious place. It was exhilarating for me to travel with my father and uncle from our small town of a few hundred people to the big city 130 miles north, where they sold mules and shopped wholesale for our mercantile supplies. I recall standing in awe at the order counter in the huge Sears, Roebuck building and crossing Ponce de Leon, to cheer for the Atlanta Crackers baseball team.

I later visited Atlanta with my high school class, touring places such as the capitol and the Cyclorama. However, it wasn't until college that I spent more time in the city. After my freshman year at Georgia Southwestern College in Americus, I transferred to Georgia Tech, where I lived in the dormitory adjacent to Tech Stadium. Having no car, I walked or rode the streetcar. I sometimes ventured downtown, but mostly lived the monastic life of a student.

Time passed, routing me to my first of two terms in the state senate in 1962. Rather than establishing a home in the capital, I stayed in the old Henry Grady Hotel. I usually left our family car in Plains for my wife, Rosalynn, who was caring for our three children and couldn't accompany me to Atlanta very often. So I walked every day from downtown to the capitol, gaining "sidewalk" insight about the community — something I recommend to anyone who really wants to explore a big city. The people, the buildings, the perspective — all become very personal when you're on foot.

During the 1960s, Atlanta was seen as the beacon of racial enlightenment throughout the Southeast. The guiding influence of the Atlanta Journal Constitution, Ralph McGill, and some fine mayors such as Ivan Allen Jr. helped Atlanta send a clear signal throughout Georgia — and throughout the South — that we should overcome the devastating effects of both legal and practical racial segregation.

And it was in this decade that the state senate began considering legislation that acquainted me more with Atlanta's poverty and racial segregation. I began to realize there were two Atlantas — the one where the decision makers lived in decent homes, with good jobs and access to good schools, and the other in low-income areas, where people often lacked medical care and sound education or even basic necessities such as food and shelter. This realization continued to grow throughout my tenure as governor, which began in 1971, and marked the only period that I lived full-time in Atlanta.

After serving as president, I returned to Plains to farm and see how I might continue to foster human rights, peace, democracy, and freedom. Rosalynn and I decided to create a nonprofit, politically neutral institution that could cut through governmental barriers or bureaucratic red tape and tackle, directly and forthrightly, the causes of personal suffering.

Several universities nationwide offered us teaching positions and the opportunity to establish a center for peace, but we wanted to stay in Georgia. Atlanta is home to many fine colleges and universities, and we were pleased to accept an offer to become part of the Emory University community. So with the help of many like-minded individuals we established The Carter Center in one room of the Emory library in late 1982.

I joined the faculty as a distinguished professor, lecturing in all schools and colleges of the university, which I continue to do today. Rosalynn became a distinguished fellow at Emory's Institute for Women's Studies, where she joins with other prominent women to discuss national and international issues.

Our Center started with just a few employees, but with many big ideas and dreams. By 1985, we had raised enough money to start building The Carter Center, along with the Presidential Library and Museum, between the Emory campus and downtown Atlanta. (We later donated the Library and Museum to the federal government, which operates it under the auspices of the National Archives.) Legend has it that our location, on Copenhill, is where General William Tecumseh Sherman watched Atlanta burn during the Civil War. Rosalynn and I are pleased that it is now a place from which we can contribute to the city's building and further development — socially, economically, and intellectually.

Although Plains is still home, we have a small apartment at the Center. With so many ties to Atlanta, it's hard not to feel that we also belong here. I often stand at our apartment's window, which overlooks 35 acres of rolling hills, gardens, and lakes, and marvel at the spectacular skyline. This city truly has come into its own.

But amid the splendor, unprecedented prosperity, and growth, we realized upon our return in the mid-1980s that Atlanta still suffered from devastating social ills, like most major urban centers in this country. These included many issues we wanted to address as private citizens — poverty, racial injustice, the drug culture, high infant mortality rates, and limited access to basic services.

From its inception, The Carter Center was dedicated to advancing peace and health worldwide, and our work today is conducted in 65 nations. We have negotiated cease-fires in places such as Bosnia,

Haiti, and Sudan, and have monitored and mediated critical elections in emerging democracies in Asia, Africa and Latin America. In some of these same nations, we have programs that prevent devastating diseases and teach farmers to increase crop production. Rather than give handouts, create large bureaucracies, or duplicate other organizations' efforts, Center staff provides people with the tools and knowledge to make changes in their own lives.

For more than two decades, The Carter Center has worked mostly in other countries. But in the early 1990s, I sensed there would be no better place to further practice The Carter Center's mission than right here in our own backyard. In many ways, the suffering in Atlanta's poor communities was every bit as intense as what the Center encountered in impoverished or war-torn countries.

So, in 1992, Rosalynn and I initiated the Atlanta Project, a program to help bridge the divide between the two Atlantas — rich and poor. In 20 neighborhoods in the city's neediest areas, we asked residents how we could help and gave them the opportunity to invite us into their lives. Next, we enticed corporations to form individual partnerships with these communities and to work closely with the residents to find lasting improvements to major problems that they identified. We trained community volunteers, and we persuaded institutions of higher education to form partnerships with the communities. While targeting improvements in housing, crime, health care, and job skills, we opened lines of communication and established bonds of trust between the two groups of Atlantans, who lived in separate worlds.

The project's initial phase was only five years, encouraging people to be independent and find ways to help themselves. During this time, many of those 20 communities, in effect, graduated from us, while others required more help. So we extended this work for three years to the fall of 1999, and today there is a legacy of community partnerships with corporations and educational institutions throughout Atlanta, bringing permanent benefits. While no one answer can "cure" society's ills, Atlantans have decided that the only real failure is to stop trying.

Atlanta in the new millenium has vitality and influence, and is prospering socially and economically. Delta, Coke, UPS, and other businesses large and small are forging models of corporate social responsibility as well as economic leadership, and the success of the universities here is outstanding. All of these things are a credit and benefit to the people of Atlanta, the state of Georgia, and the entire region.

And let's not forget our world-famous Braves and up-and-coming Falcons. Our major sports teams raise our collective spirit and introduce Atlanta to the rest of the country.

GO ATLANTA!

Former U.S. President Jimmy Carter, recipient of the 2002 Nobel Peace Prize, chairs the nonprofit Carter Center in Atlanta.

CITYSCAPE & neighborhoods

The Westin Peachtree Plaza hotel in downtown Atlanta's skyline
©*Atlantaphotos.com*

The dazzling lights of Atlanta's skyline
©*Atlantaphotos.com*

1100 Peachtree, midtown Atlanta

The towering buildings represent the growth of a modern city.

Centennial Olympic Park
Photo provided by the Atlanta Convention and Visitors Bureau

For over 25 years, the Metropolitan Atlanta Rapid Transit Authority has been serving the community.
Photo provided by the Atlanta Convention and Visitors Bureau, courtesy Kelly Mills for MARTA

SunTrust Plaza, currently the second tallest building in Atlanta, was designed by John Portman & Associates.

The dramatic atrium lobby of Marriott Marquis in downtown Atlanta
©*Atlantaphotos.com*

Georgia World Congress Center entry with downtown skyline
©*Atlantaphotos.com*

Atlanta's Hard Rock Cafe is situated in downtown Atlanta's Cornerstone Building.

(Opposite page) Centennial Olympic Park, located in the heart of downtown Atlanta,
is a popular destination for visitors from all around the world.

(Above) Centennial Olympic Park is an urban oasis featuring 21 acres of lush lawns, cascading water gardens,
covered pavilions, an amphitheater and five quilt plazas telling the story of Atlanta's Olympic Games.

Centennial Olympic Park

Entry to Underground Atlanta with fountain and downtown skyline
©Atlantaphotos.com

Children love playing in the water at Centennial Olympic Park Fountain.
©*Atlantaphotos.com*

(Above) International Plaza at the Georgia World Congress Center in downtown
©*Atlantaphotos.com*

Piedmont Park field
©*Atlantaphotos.com*

Martin Luther King Jr. Freedom March down Auburn Avenue
©Atlantaphotos.com

Carnegie monument at Hardy Ivy Park on Peachtree Street in downtown Atlanta
©Atlantaphotos.com

After creating a statue of Southern Railway's first president, Samuel Spencer, sculptor Daniel C. French went on to make the Lincoln Memorial.

Colony Square apartments in midtown viewed from across Peachtree Street
©Atlantaphotos.com

(Above) Completed in 1889, the Classical Renaissance architecture of Georgia's State Capitol resembles that of the United States Capitol.

Georgia State Capitol with tulips in the Spring
©Atlantaphotos.com

Original sculptures are highlighted throughout downtown Atlanta.

PHOTOGRAPHY CORSON DESIGN DIMENSIONAL ARTS EMRAY, INC. McDONALDS COPPER MOON KIESGEN
565

Decorative pillars stand prominently in front of the SunTrust Bank.

Little Five Points, located between Greenwich Village and the French Quarter, has a rich mix of art, theater and commerce.

Marietta is a nice place for people of all ages to spend the day.
Marietta Welcome Center and Visitors Bureau, Marietta, GA

Storefronts in Virginia Highland neighborhood
©*Atlantaphotos.com*

A Buckhead home is surrounded by Atlanta's display of spring flowering trees.
©Atlantaphotos.com

Located two miles east of downtown, Historic Inman Park is Atlanta's first planned community and one of the nation's first garden suburbs. It is listed on the National Register of Historic Places.
© *Atlantaphotos.com*

The houses are as diverse as its inhabitants in Inman Park.

ARTS & entertainment

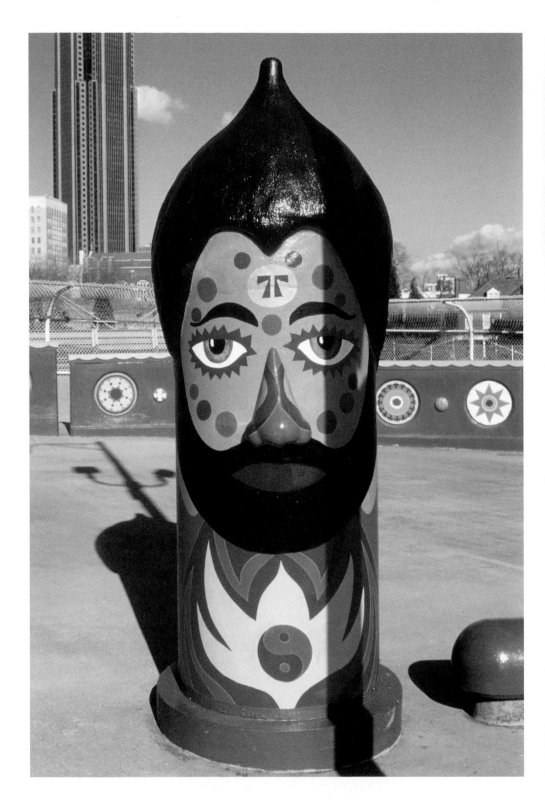

Atlanta's diversity and culture is evident in the roadside art.

The Primitive Eye Gallery has a wonderful array of folk art tucked away in an older home situated among Scottsdale's area of art galleries and antique shops.

High Museum of Art with Calder mobile
©*Atlantaphotos.com*

The High Museum of Art's current home is an award-winning building designed by noted architect Richard Meier. It opened to worldwide acclaim in 1983. The building has received many design awards since then, including a 1991 citation from the American Institute of Architects as one of the "10 best works of American architecture of the 1980s."

Atlanta Cyclorama is home to one of the world's great cyclorama paintings.
The immense painting, completed in 1885, depicts the Civil War Battle of Atlanta.
©*Atlantaphotos.com*

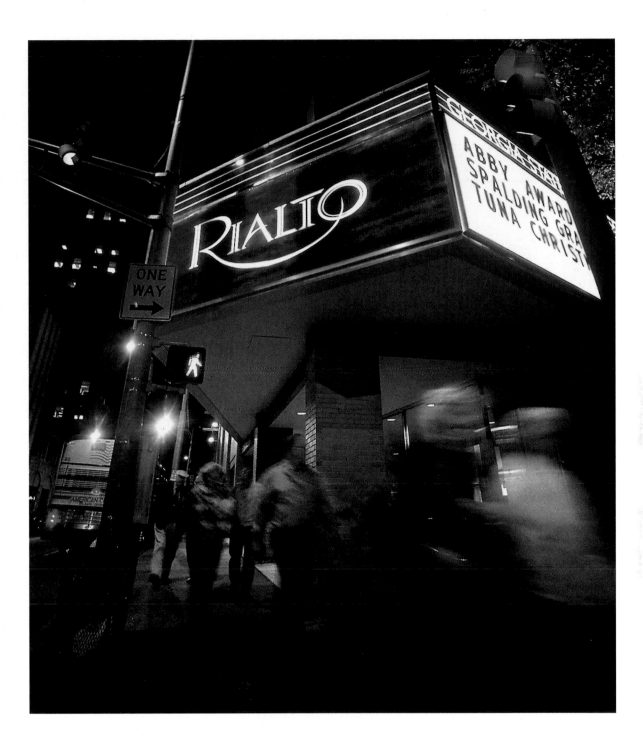

The Rialto Center for the Performing Arts, Georgia State University
Courtesy of Georgia State University

The Fox Theatre was almost demolished in the 1970s to make way for a skyscraper.

Looking out from the Fox Theatre stage where a wide array of productions are performed
©*Atlantaphotos.com*

(Spread) Interior and exterior of Fox Theatre
Photo by Michael Portman, courtesy of Fox Theatre

Music Director Robert Spano conducts the Atlanta Symphony Orchestra.
Courtesy of JD Scott and the Atlanta Symphony Orchestra

Atlanta Symphony Orchestra performing at the Woodruff Arts Center
©Atlantaphotos.com

"Thunder River" at Six Flags over Georgia is a white water rafting adventure for the whole family.
©*Atlantaphotos.com*

"The Georgia Scorcher" at Six Flags over Georgia is one of the Southeast's tallest and fastest stand-up rollercoasters.
© *Atlantaphotos.com*

Centennial Olympic Park hosts a variety of events throughout the year
including a Fourth of July celebration, concerts and festivals, making it Atlanta's gathering place.
Centennial Olympic Park

Vendors display their goods from around the world at the Black Arts Festival.
© *Atlantaphotos.com*

The Omni Hotel located at CNN Center in downtown Atlanta, just across the street from Centennial Olympic Park.
©Atlantaphotos.com

CNN's "Talk Back Live" program in action at CNN Center
©*Atlantaphotos.com*

LIFESTYLE

The Varsity is recognized as the world's largest drive-in restaurant.

The Big Chicken at KFC on Cobb Parkway in Marietta
Marietta Welcome Center and Visitors Bureau, Marietta, GA

A sixty-five-foot copper fish sculpture outside Buckhead's Fishmarket restaurant
© *Atlantaphotos.com*

(Top row, left and center) For three decades, Woody has been doling out a hunk of his hometown in every Philly cheese steak he makes.

(Bottom row, left) As much a saloon as a restaurant, Buffalo's Cafe puts its focus on fun and entertainment.

(Top row, right) Java Jive is a fun mix of colorful chrome, vintage kitchenware and Formica tables.

(Bottom row, center) Clermont Lounge defies simple classification. Part dive bar, part strip club, the Clermont is where in- and out-of-towners go more for the mystique than the show.

(Bottom row, right) Krispy Kreme Doughnuts offers 24-hour drive-thru service.

Maggiano's Italian restaurant on Peachtree Street in the heart of Buckhead
© *Atlantaphotos.com*

Outside dining in Virginia Highland cafe
© *Atlantaphotos.com*

DeKalb Market features a little of just about everything. Covering more than two football fields worth of space, the stock represents the best of the produce of regional farmers.

True to its mission, the market is staffed by friendly people from all over the world, who wear tags with their name, country of origin and the languages they speak.

Phipps Plaza in Buckhead is almost entirely devoted to upscale stores.
©*Atlantaphotos.com*

Entry to Atlanta's Lenox Square shopping center in Buckhead
© *Atlantaphotos.com*

Robinson College of Business at Georgia State University
Courtesy of Georgia State University

(Top row, left) Helen M. Aderhold Learning Center at Georgia State University

(Bottom row) The Student Center (left) and the Library (right) are popular hangouts at Georgia State University

All photos courtesy of Georgia State University

(Top row, left) The Emory University Haygood Hopkins Gate is the main entrance to the campus.

(Top row, right) Glenn United Methodist Church on the Emory University campus

(Bottom row, left) Emory University class meets on a Spring afternoon on the Emory Quadrangle.

(Bottom row, right) Pitts Theology Library of Emory University surrounded by fall colors

Emory University

(Top row, left) Emory University's George and Irene Woodruff Residential Hall on Clifton Road

(Top row, right) Emory University Candler Library (in foreground) sits at the north end of the Quadrangle. Downtown Atlanta is visible in the background.

(Bottom row) Emory University's Woodruff Physical Education Center track and soccer field

Emory University

Henry Grady High School, established in 1947, is located just south of Piedmont Park in Atlanta's vibrant Midtown section. Named for Henry W. Grady, editor of *The Atlanta Constitution* and a proponent of a "New South" in the post-Civil War era, Grady High School has a long tradition of producing proficient leaders for Atlanta.

The Shrine of North America, Yaarab Shrine, is known for its colorful parades, circuses and clowns. But there is also a serious side to this international fraternity of approximately 500,000 men belonging to 191 Shrine Temples, or chapters, throughout North America. For 75 years, the Shrine has operated a network of specialized hospitals that treat children with orthopedic problems, burns and spinal cord injuries, up to their 18th birthday, free of charge.

(Above and center)
The first Eucharistic Celebration of Christ the King Parish was held on
August 15, 1936, in celebration of the Feast of The Assumption. The Parish
was established by Bishop Gerald P. O'Hara on June 15, 1936.

The Cathedral of St. Philip, the oldest Episcopal parish in Atlanta,
is one of the largest parishes in the country with over 5,500 active participants.

First Baptist Church Atlanta offers services and Bible sessions in English and
Spanish several days a week.

Ebenezer Baptist Church, the sanctuary where Dr. Martin Luther King Jr. was baptized and later preached, is in the first phase of a multi-million-dollar project to restore the three-story red-brick structure to its 1960s appearance.

The Temple has served as a center for Atlanta's Jewish cultural, educational and social activities since its construction in 1931. It is the home of the city's oldest Jewish congregation – the Hebrew Benevolent Society, established in 1860 to serve the needs of the local German-Jewish immigrants.

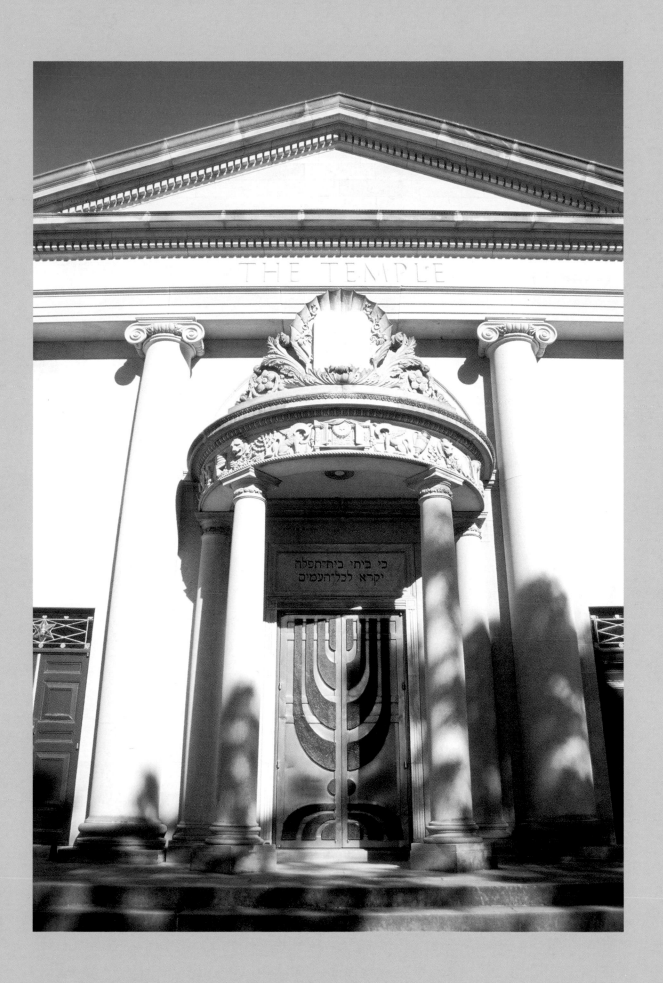

Oakland Cemetery, established in 1850, is Oakland-Atlanta's oldest cemetery and it is a supreme
example of a Victorian cemetery. The layout, as well as the monuments,
speaks of the history of their time through symbolic interpretation.

Mute reminders of the past abound in Oakland Cemetery including the mighty Confederate Lion which stands guard over the Confederate grounds. Amidst the monuments is a broad and fascinating 150-year history of Atlanta and its environs.

SPORTS &
recreation

Turner Field

The fans at Turner Field

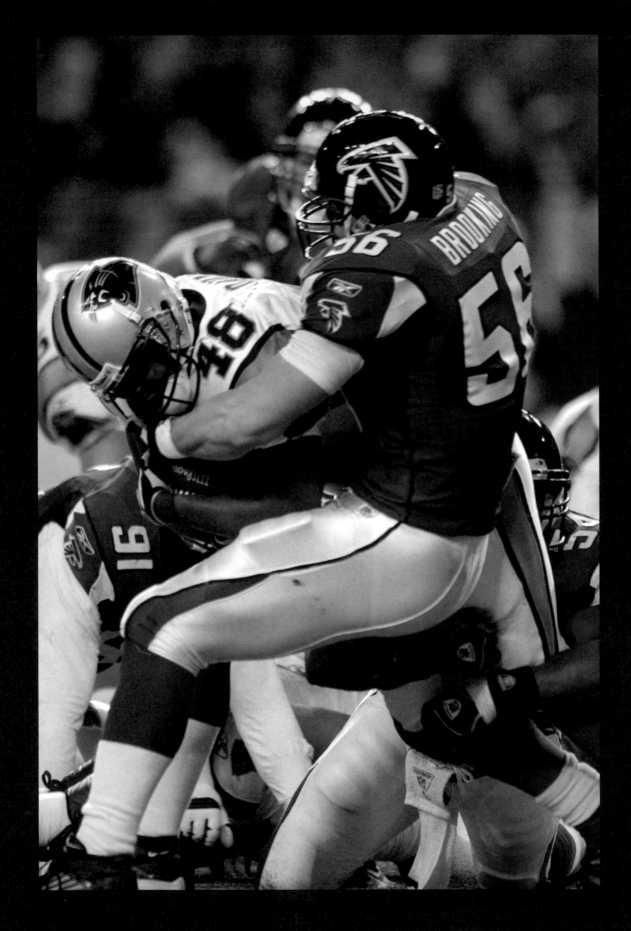

Linebacker Keith Brooking had 212 total tackles in 2002.
Atlanta Falcons

Michael Vick, Quarterback of the Atlanta Falcons, became only the sixth quarterback to be voted
to the NFL All-Star game in his first year as a starter.
Atlanta Falcons

(Opposite page) The interior of the Georgia Dome with the Falcons in play

(Above) The Georgia Dome illuminated in the early evening, located in downtown Atlanta

Philips Arena, with its seating capacity of 20,000+, is home to Atlanta Hawks, the Atlanta Thrashers, and the Georgia Force.
©Atlantaphotos.com

Atlanta Hawks court at Philips Arena
Scott Cunningham/NBAE/Getty Images

(Opposite page) Thrashers Forward Ilya Kovalchuk

(Above) Thrashers Forward Dany Heatley

(Next spread) Thrashers bench forwards, Marc Savard, Dany Heatley and Ilya Kovalchuk

Courtesy of Scott Cunningham/Atlanta Thrashers

Georgia Tech's nationally prominent basketball team plays its home games on campus at
Alexander Memorial Coliseum at McDonald's Center. The 9,191-seat arena is known as the "Thriller Dome."
Stanley Leary

Nestled in the heart of midtown, Georgia Tech's Bobby Dodd Stadium at Historic Grant Field is easily one of the nation's most unique venues for college football. Originally built in 1913, it is the oldest on-campus stadium in NCAA Division I-A, and recent renovation raised its capacity to 55,000.

Scott Cunningham

(Top) Victory is always a cause for celebration, but is even sweeter in events like the prestigious Petit Le Mans at Road Atlanta, a 1,000-mile endurance test of man and machine. (Bottom) Road Atlanta is a world class 2.54-mile, 12-turn road course located on 700 park-like acres in Northeast Georgia.
Road Atlanta/David Allio

(Top) Le Mans Prototypes like the Audi R8 are the fastest and most exotic sports cars that race in the Petit Le Mans at Road Atlanta. (Bottom) Corvette is a leading contender in the GTS class of American Le Mans Series races like the Petit Le Mans at Road Atlanta.
Road Atlanta/David Allio

The many scenic pathways in Atlanta make jogging more enjoyable.

PLACES
to see

(Spread) The World of Coca-Cola® Atlanta, adjacent to Underground Atlanta, has over 1,000 articles of memorabilia telling the story of the popular soft drink. Visitors can sample over 40 domestic and international beverages.
©*Atlantaphotos.com*

The Mountaintop skylift's cable cars climb 825 feet above Stone Mountain.
©*Atlantaphotos.com*

(Above, top) Stone Mountain's tour trains take visitors on a 5-mile journey around the base of the enormous mountain.

(Above, bottom) Carving in granite on side of Stone Mountain

Tullie Smith House

ca. 1845
DeKalb County, Georgia

The exact date of the house remains unknown, but it was most likely constructed between 1845 and 1850. It was originally located amidst 800 acres on what is now North Druid Hills Road in Atlanta. Tullie Smith House is typical of the southern rural home of the mid-19th century, with its exterior end chimneys, hall and parlor plan, full-width porch, and traveler's room. The traveler's (or parson's) room remained unlocked for visitors, who could enter at any time without disturbing the family. A variety of activities, such as carding and spinning wool, weaving, preparing food, and washing would have occurred in the house and on the porch, depending upon the time of year and the family's needs.

(Spread) A plantation-plain house built in the late 1840s by the Robert Smith family, Tullie Smith House is listed on the National Register of Historic Places. Originally located east of Atlanta, outside the city limits, the house survived the near-total destruction of Atlanta in 1864. The original first floor plan was altered c. 1875, but it has been restored. By the late 1960s, Atlanta's highways and executive park developments mushroomed around this house. Heirs offered to donate the house and kitchen outbuilding to the Atlanta Historical Society (now the Atlanta History Center), and an Atlanta banker provided the money needed for their relocation in 1969 and restoration in the early 1970s.

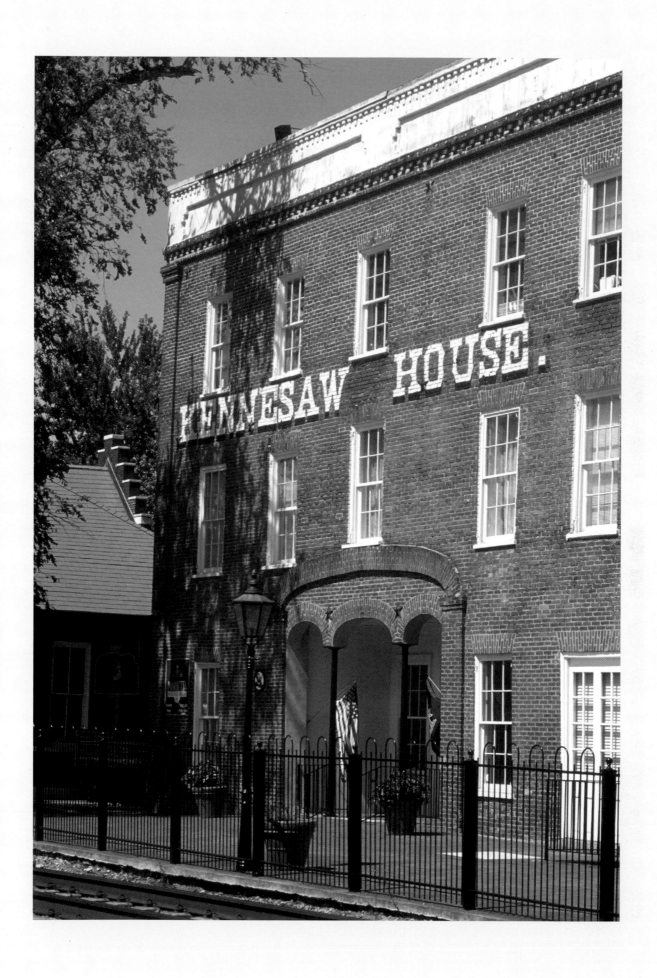

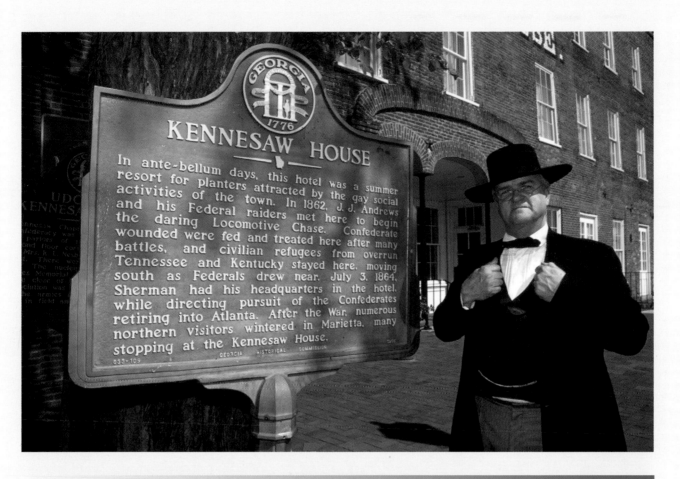

KENNESAW HOUSE

In ante-bellum days, this hotel was a summer resort for planters attracted by the gay social activities of the town. In 1862, J. J. Andrews and his Federal raiders met here to begin the daring Locomotive Chase. Confederate wounded were fed and treated here after many battles, and civilian refugees from overrun Tennessee and Kentucky stayed here, moving south as Federals drew near. July 3, 1864, Sherman had his headquarters in the hotel, while directing pursuit of the Confederates retiring into Atlanta. After the War, numerous northern visitors wintered in Marietta, many stopping at the Kennesaw House.

(Top and opposite page) The Kennesaw House is now home to the Marietta Museum of History.

(Bottom) Kennesaw Mountain National Battlefield

Marietta Welcome Center and Visitors Bureau, Marietta, GA

Marietta's Fire Museum
Marietta Welcome Center and Visitors Bureau, Marietta, GA

The Train Depot was built for the second time in 1898. It is now home to the Marietta Welcome Center and Visitors Bureau.
Marietta Welcome Center and Visitors Bureau, Marietta, GA

(Spread) Marietta Square is set around a lushly landscaped park.
Marietta Welcome Center and Visitors Bureau, Marietta, GA

The Fuqua Conservatory at Atlanta Botanical Garden displays plants in tropical and desert environments
with an emphasis on rare, threatened or endangered plants.
(Top photo) © *Atlantaphotos.com*

Small but exquisite, the Japanese garden is one of the oldest areas of the Atlanta Botanical Garden. The meditation garden contains the "three old friends" typically found in a Japanese garden: pine and/or stone which symbolize longevity and age, bamboo which is symbolic of resilience in the face of adversity and blooming fruit trees which represent youth and renewal of life.

The Atlanta Botanical Garden features 15 acres of outdoor display gardens.

Zoo Atlanta has been rated one of the 10 best zoos in the country.
Photos by Joe Sebo, ©Zoo Atlanta

(Above) Fernbank Museum of Natural History is the only natural history museum in the world located in a natural environment.
(Following pages) Fernbank Museum atrium with owls
©Atlantaphotos.com

Chateau Elan resort and golf club
©*Atlantaphotos.com*

"Tranquilla," one of Marietta's antebellum treasures, was a model for Tara in "Gone with the Wind."
Marietta Welcome Center and Visitors Bureau, Marietta, GA

The Margaret Mitchell House and "Gone With the Wind" Museum offer a look into the life of the renowned author and a chance to revisit Atlanta in 1939 for the three-day gala that surrounded the premier of the movie made from the book Mitchell wrote.

The Wren's Nest historic house museum
© *Atlantaphotos.com*

Atlanta History Center, home of The Swan House, The Tullie Smith House and
museum of Atlanta's history including the history of the Civil War
© *Atlantaphotos.com*

Historic classical mansion of Atlanta's first black millionare, Alonzo Franklin Herndon
©Atlantaphotos.com

Georgia's Governor's Mansion on W. Paces Ferry Road in Buckhead
©Atlantaphotos.com

Established in 1968 by Coretta Scott King, The King Center is the official, living memorial dedicated to the advancement of the legacy of Dr. Martin Luther King, Jr., leader of America's greatest nonviolent movement for justice, equality and peace.

More than 650,000 visitors from all over the world are drawn annually to the King Center to pay homage to Dr. King, view unique exhibits illustrating his life and teachings and visit the King Center's Library, Archives, his final resting place, his birth home, gift shop and other facilities.

Birth place of Martin Luther King, Jr.
Provided by Atlanta Convention & Visitors Bureau
Joe Cooke, National Park Service

The Carter Center includes a 69,750-square-foot library (above) and the Carter Center,
a nonprofit organization dedicated to advancing peace and health worldwide.
©*Atlantaphotos.com*

The replica of the Oval Office from the White House is in the Jimmy Carter Library & Museum.
©Atlantaphotos.com

Jimmy Carter Library entry with international flags ©Atlantaphotos.com

Robert Bowden, Inc. has always maintained a strategic goal to serve the communities where we live and work. I'm very proud not only of what our employee/partners have achieved in business, but also their zeal to support our community. The greatest impact of RBI may be our quiet financial and physical support of the community and the vast individual charitable acts of our many partners.

Steve Cole, President
Robert Bowden, Inc.

BUILDING A GREATER ATLANTA

Architecture, construction and landscape industries shape tomorrow's city,
providing working and living space for area residents.

Perkins & Will

Nationally and internationally recognized for its achievements in architecture, interior design and planning, Perkins & Will is the firm of choice for health care, higher education, K-12, science & technology, corporate and civic architecture, and interiors. Since 1935 Perkins & Will has worked with some of the world's leading companies and institutions. With each client — from the neighborhood elementary school to the Fortune 100 corporate campus to the most advanced biomedical research facility — Perkins & Will learns and evolves creatively and professionally.

Through solid relationships, Perkins & Will creates spaces that make their mark and enhance daily life. Its people — some 750 — are enthusiasts. They are passionate about their work and driven to achieve the vision of their clients. Perkins & Will is structured according to practice as well as location to ensure every project succeeds with the best possible collection of talent and experience. As a unified collaborative firm practicing in regional centers, it is always close to its clients. Working out of offices in Atlanta, Boston, Calgary, Chicago, Charlotte, Dallas, Houston, Los Angeles, Miami, Minneapolis, Research Triangle Park, Seattle, New York, Beijing, Shanghai and Vancouver, Perkins &

Will has completed projects in 49 states and 40 countries around the globe.

Perkins & Will's Atlanta office was established in 1977 as Nix Mann and Associates, a firm specializing in health care design. Nix Mann Viehman Architects was founded in 1986 when the practice diversified into non-health care markets, including a wide range of educational facilities, libraries, teaching and research laboratories and offices.

In 1995 Perkins & Will merged with Nix Mann and Associates and Nix Mann Viehman Architects to form what

(Right)
Pearlman Cancer Center, South Georgia Medical Center, Valdosta, Georgia
Photo by William Nelson

(Below left)
J. Erskine Love, Jr. Manufacturing Building at the Georgia Institute of Technology in Atlanta, Georgia
Photo by Jonathan Hillyer Photography Inc./ Esto Photographers Inc.

(Below right)
Whitefield Academy, Atlanta, Georgia
Photo by Tod Swiecichowski for Switch Photo

is now Perkins & Will in Atlanta. The merger brought Perkins & Will's nationally recognized health care and education expertise together with the established health care, academic, government and corporate practice in Atlanta. The office currently has a staff of 134 and is located on Peachtree Street in Midtown Atlanta in a restored historic home.

Enduring creativity is the essence of architecture and design. Perkins & Will works with that goal in mind — to craft ideas and create buildings that honor the broader goals of society while meeting the everyday needs of those who live, work and aspire within those spaces. Spanning nearly 70 years Perkins & Will has forged a heritage of exceptional service and design excellence. Routinely recognized as one of the nation's most-respected design firms, its body of work features some of the most significant architectural accomplishments of last century. In the past decade alone Perkins & Will is the only design practice in the country to receive seven national Design Honor Awards, including the industry's highest honor, the American Institute of Architects' Firm of the Year Award.

(Top left)
Children's Healthcare of Atlanta AFLAC Cancer Center
Photo by Chris A. Little Photography

(Top right)
Centennial Place YMCA, Atlanta, Georgia
Photo by Creative Sources Photography, Inc.

(Left)
Cox Hall Student Center at Emory University in Atlanta, Georgia
Photo by Tod Swiecichowski for Switch Photo

(Right)
McKinsey and Company, Atlanta, Georgia
Photo by Gary Knight & Associates Photography, Inc.

Robert Bowden, Inc.

Headquartered in Marietta, Georgia, Robert Bowden, Inc. is an employee-owned wholesale building material supply and manufacturing company. The company, best known for windows, doors, and millwork, distributes to professional builders in the Atlanta metropolitan area.

Robert Bowden, Inc., which now has total revenue of nearly $110 million and 330 employees, is organized around the concept of "intrepreneurship" — managers running small companies with the protection and support of a much larger organization. This strategy assures a strong focus on the customer and a firm grip on the details

(Left)
Senior Management
Team from L-R
Nick Massengill,
Greg Lucas, Bert
Bowden, Steve Cole,
Chris Rogers, Mark Cole,
Jim Turriglio,
Steve LeCroy.

(Right)
Window
Production Line

The headquarters and manufacturing facility are located in the shadows of historic Kennesaw Mountain where on June 27, 1864, a battle raged between the Union forces of William Tecumseh Sherman and the Confederate forces of General Joseph Johnston. The Union forces could not win the field that day because the mountain and Confederate troops stood too formidable. On June 27, 1983, exactly 119 years after the battle, Robert Bowden and Steve Cole formed a company that would become a formidable institution of its own. The soldiers on both sides of the Battle of Kennesaw Mountain displayed a strong commitment and a belief in their cause. Similarly, the team at Robert Bowden, Inc. has also marched on with a strong commitment against present-day odds.

The company's humble beginnings started with a 20,000-square-foot lease of a former Ryder truck rental facility, a couple of trucks and a strong business philosophy. Today the company operates 60 trucks shipping out of branches located in Marietta, Duluth and McDonough, Georgia. More than 55 percent of the products sold by the company go through the manufacturing and fabrication facility, located in Marietta. All together the company has over 350,000 square feet of warehouse located on 25 acres of real estate.

of the business. Each branch, division and department is organized into a small company inside a company. These smaller entities make decisions, budget, take risks and are rewarded based on performance. This environment values individual contribution, encourages innovation and stimulates team members to consider the impact of decisions on the customer.

The company operates four sales divisions organized around the individual needs of the customer group being served. The Architectural Products Division represents products that are found in some of the largest and most elaborate homes built in Atlanta. The Merchant Builder Division has products that can be found in the homes of the top 25 volume builders in town. The Custom Builder Division stays focused on customers that may not build very many units, but are very interested in service and details. The staff of the Contractor Sales Division serves most other professional customers.

The Robert Bowden, Inc. vision, "To create the future with people who are uncompromising in their passion for excellence," speaks volumes about the organization. "Our competitive advantage," says Steve Cole, president of Robert Bowden, Inc., "is firmly rooted in our ability to understand our customer and our desire to make it happen." This is a company where average is considered sub-standard and the best way to predict the future is to invent it.

Touring the Robert Bowden, Inc. facilities makes a couple of things very clear. This isn't your grandparents' lumberyard and these aren't your typical building material people. Plenty of signs, literature and bulletin boards reinforce the same message that "self-help" business books, typically found in local bookstores, communicate. The dispatcher at one of the branches, also an Employee Ownership Committee member, comments, "We absolutely believe this stuff, look what we've accomplished!" Robert Bowden, Inc. has posted a 20-year record of 18 percent compounded growth, while competing with national companies in a highly competitive, turbulent and often consolidating industry.

Robert Bowden, Inc. employees are different. The energy level is high and everyone seems to move briskly. In fact, these employees own the company. From the very beginning, the company has had a philosophy of sharing the success with employees. But in December of 2001 the previous owners took a big leap and sold the company to the employees that had helped build it. The total ownership of the company is being transferred to the employees through an Employee Stock Ownership Plan (ESOP). An ESOP is a tax-qualified retirement program that actually owns the company and transitions the stock to the employees as a long-term benefit. The employees earn stock through "sweat equity." Nick Massengill, Vice President of Sales & Marketing, said, "The ESOP is reinforcing ownership values and ultimately maintaining and growing a culture that understands and values our customers." The company's competitors are forced to compete with employees that are motivated and come to work thinking like owners.

Robert Bowden, Inc. operates a fleet of more than 60 delivery and service vehicles.

The company has not labored in obscurity. Quite the contrary — it is well-known in industry circles and has earned numerous local, regional and national awards. Among them is the prestigious National Dealer of the Year Award, presented by the influential publishing company, Hanley-Wood, Inc., publisher of *Builder* magazine. In addition, Robert Bowden, Inc. has received the Small Business of the Year Award presented by the Cobb County Chamber of Commerce; the Gazelle Award for the Fastest Growing Companies in Atlanta presented by the *Atlanta Business Chronicle* and Robinson Humphrey; and the Dealer of the Year Award for Georgia and Alabama by the Construction Suppliers Association.

Bowden has also earned countless other accolades for its valued approach to doing business. Some of the recent notable honors include the Top 50 Entrepreneurs in Atlanta presented by *Catalyst* magazine and the 2003 Consumer Choice Award for Business Excellence. Robert Bowden, Inc. has been recognized as one of the Top 100 Manufacturers in the country by *Window and Door* magazine; the 58th largest construction supplier to the professional builder by *ProSales* magazine; and the 74th largest building supplier — where the list included retailers like Home Depot — by *ProDealer* magazine. Steve Cole notes, "These recognitions serve to confirm the philosophy, commitment, hard work and dedication of all of Robert Bowden's employee-partners."

Robert Bowden, Inc. has certainly been a company to watch over the last 20 years. One can't help but believe that the past may serve as just a glimpse of what might be possible for this dynamic organization in the future. Robert Bowden, Inc. is living its vision, "To Create the Future with People Who Are Uncompromising in their Passion for Excellence."

(Left)
Custom Millwork Department

(Right)
Interior Door Assmebly

Piedmont Landscape

Atlanta enjoys one of the most diverse climates in the country. Located in the Piedmont geographical region of the southeastern United States, Atlanta experiences the fullness of all four seasons of the year. In this area it is possible to cultivate select plants from sub-tropical climates to a few that are found in Alpine settings far to the north. In Atlanta, it is not uncommon to see Windmill Palms growing next to Canadian Hemlocks! As one can imagine, this brings many challenges in the culture of these plants. The hot, humid summers bring various plant diseases to its shrubs, trees and turf while the bitter cold arctic blasts that occur once or twice in the winter can cause problems as well. Having the book and field knowledge to properly select materials, diagnose problems and remedy them is a complex and challenging effort. Piedmont Landscape is well equipped for that challenge.

Founded in 1999, Piedmont Landscape has assembled a team of managers, supervisors, and crew persons that are second-to-none in the industry. With backgrounds as diverse as Atlanta itself, the Piedmont team brings decades of combined landscape experience and customer service to work every day.

A horticulture industry leader, Piedmont Landscape utilizes exemplary management styles and concepts for landscaping projects within industrial, commercial, residential, and multi-family communities. By combining quality and superior customer service, the company exceeds its clients' requirements as they have ideally visualized them.

For commercial maintenance, Piedmont believes in initiating and engaging the complete management of its customers' landscapes. While servicing these customers, Piedmont provides a crew of landscapers that does not alter from day to day. This consistency is also reflected in its same-day service policy. In addition, the company conducts monthly inspections that identify issues related to the property's overall state of health and improvements that might be necessary, such as new plantings, irrigation services, and arbor care.

Piedmont also provides the architect, owner, developer, or general contractor with many years of commercial construction experience. Specifically, the company's familiarity with industrial, municipal and multi-family project management shapes a Piedmont Landscape Team ready to serve its customers with great proficiency. This team understands the vital importance of deadlines as well as the integrity of an aesthetically gratifying and appropriately installed landscape.

Once Piedmont comprehends its clients' visions, it uses industry know-how and skillfulness to make them a reality. In the area of floriculture, Piedmont works with clients to determine the most tailor-fit color to match their properties' individual needs. Once the company has maximized its clients' curb appeal and increased traffic flow, it makes sure to continually monitor and maintain its properties' colors throughout the seasons to endorse their attractiveness and appeal.

Piedmont's specialized landscape designers and personalized maintenance programs also enable clients to creatively customize their properties. With its wide inventory of containers, pots, and hanging baskets, Piedmont supplies various products that help properties' shine with all of the charm and health that a landscape should retain.

Piedmont Landscape treats the land that it tends to — no matter what its classification — with the respect and care that nature deserves. By taking the time to talk to its clients about their landscaping wishes, the company assesses, develops, finishes, and monitors the work that it has done — all in the name of horticulture enrichment.

"With more than 40 years of experience and a strong global presence, LeasePlan has forged its place as a leader in the fleet management industry. LeasePlan USA manages more than 400,000 vehicles for clients nationwide including local Atlanta Fortune 500 organizations. Our employees and our dedication to quality service have made LeasePlan a leading Atlanta company."

David G. Dahm, President and CEO
LeasePlan USA

With its position as the financial center of the Southeast and its emerging niche in the global arena, Atlanta has seen a rise in entrepreneurial ventures and small businesses. By partnering with small business owners, National Financial Services Group provides access to services and products that will enhance and increase both their business success and their financial futures.

Atlanta also offers a wealth of family-friendly resources that reflect our philosophy of the balanced lifestyle so important to everyone.

National Financial Services Group is enthusiastic about our role in Atlanta's bright future.

James L. Cook, Jr., ChFC, CFS
National Financial Services Group

BUSINESS & FINANCE

A wide array of Atlanta companies and institutions contribute to the financial growth, security and success of scores of local and international individuals and companies.

Alliance Royale

VALUE TO CLIENTS, PROFESSIONALS AND THE COMMUNITY

When Alliance Royale comes into a community, its impact is subtle but effective and powerful — reaching deep into the community to help its citizens build and sustain themselves as individuals, as well as the community as a whole. Its objective is to change the way people plan their finances, career/business, and their life — by educating, planning, supporting, and implementing. Although its apparent value to clients is more obvious, the business opportunity to value-based professionals is a paradigm shift in how their business can prosper within the world of Alliance Royale.

Wm. James Long, Co-Founder and CEO

SUPPORTING PEOPLE — GETTING BETTER RESULTS IN BOTH THEIR PERSONAL AND BUSINESS LIFE

Since its inception over 20 years ago, Alliance Royale has operated much like a traditional financial and training firm. Its underlying philosophy — simple, yet powerful — "supporting people in getting better results in their personal and business life, so that they may thrive, not just survive" has fueled its growth and the development of a system. This system has not only filled a void in the industry for clients but also has provided an innovative and profitable business model for value-based professionals, unmatched in the industry.

THE ALLIANCE ROYALE DIFFERENCE FINANCIAL FREEDOM, FINDING PURPOSE, AND ACHIEVING GOALS

Founders of Alliance Royale, experts in the field of financial and business services, wanted to differentiate themselves in the industry by addressing a common

frustration felt by people when they worked to develop and implement a plan in a traditional environment. Alliance Royale's passion to support people in becoming financially free, finding their purpose and achieving their goals, and helping businesses grow is the foundation of its culture. And that culture is not only the reason clients grow to rely on it, but it is also the main attraction for professionals that choose to join its Advisory team.

OUR MISSION

Alliance Royale's dedication to its mission — to provide the professional advisors, systems, and resources to create and implement life plans to support individuals in achieving financial freedom and building successful businesses — was the foundation for the Endowment Program. By devising the program, the founders could use their unparalleled expertise in advanced financial planning, which clearly set them apart in the industry.

Alliance Royale looked at the needs of churches, schools, and other nonprofit organizations focused on improving the quality of life, for them as individuals and as a community, and accepted the challenge to create a solution that worked. The Endowment Program was designed to benefit each participant and their family, their church or nonprofit organization, as well as build community centers to improve the lives of the people in each church and their community. It is the most unique program of its kind and one that significantly changes the economic foundation of many churches and nonprofit organizations and their congregations and supporters.

INTEGRATED LIFE, FINANCIAL, AND BUSINESS PLANNING

Alliance Royale's approach is refreshing in meeting life's challenges in a new and effective way. It's not about doing it faster or cheaper, but doing it in an effective way that gives its clients peace of mind, knowing that its solution meets "their" needs. Whether these needs are personal or business related, Alliance does not just focus on the short term, but on the long term as well. And it's not just about planning, it's about doing and actually supporting clients in achieving their goals. The company has branded its approach integrated life, financial, and business planning.

Whenever someone is faced with a challenge, they need to evaluate their options and determine the best ones for them based on their specific goals in life. Frustration sets in when people realize that their professional advisors do not have the capability of integrating their services into an integrated plan for them. Each of them may be experts in their field; however, their inherent business structure limits their ability to work with other service providers to ensure a provided solution does not negatively impact another area. Although it has always made sense to have an integrated plan, no one in the industry could do it effectively — until now.

Alliance Royale Advisory Center in Buckhead, located in the Monarch Plaza

VALUE PROPOSITION TO BUSINESS OWNERS

Along the way, Alliance Royale has found that its approach to integrated planning is especially critical to business owners. Due to the fact that business owners' personal and business lives are so naturally intertwined, integrated planning was absolutely critical. Alliance Royale soon became a specialist in business expansion and business transition, as its business clients increasingly relied on it to support them through the evolution of their business. Whether it is helping business owners obtain capital for business expansion, creating and implementing franchise programs, or providing professional services for buying and selling businesses and franchises, Alliance Royale is a resource business owners can rely on.

ADVISORY SERVICES — PROPRIETARY SYSTEM — INTEGRATION — EDUCATING

Alliance Royale has continually expanded its company to provide the depth and breadth of services needed to provide true integrated financial, life, and business services. Currently, it provides 16 core planning services, in themselves standard in the industry, but also more. These core planning services layer their proprietary system and environment on top, enabling its Advisory teams to develop true integrated client solutions. Its extensive background in training also gives its approach an "educating" flair. This supports its philosophy that people need to take personal responsibility for their lives and make conscious proactive decisions rather than just reacting to the day-to-day crisis that life brings — never really moving forward, or worse yet, allowing external forces to control destiny.

EXPANSION PLAN — DEVELOPING ADVISORY CENTERS AND COMMUNITY LIFE CENTERS

Alliance Royale is now in the midst of implementing an aggressive expansion plan to develop Alliance Royale Advisory Centers in key metropolitan areas across the United States. The company brings its unique brand of integrated financial, life, and business planning services to

> Alliance Royale's ambitious tag line — Changing the World of Commerce — seems ominous to most, however, the company is doing it — one life, one family, one business, and one community at a time.

clients and their communities. In addition, it provides a powerful and profitable business proposition to value-based professionals and innovative programs to support churches and non-profit organizations in achieving their outreach goals and community life centers.

Alliance Royale's ambitious tag line — Changing the World of Commerce — seems ominous to most, however, the company is doing it — one life, one family, one business, and one community at a time.

Federal Home Loan Bank of Atlanta

The Federal Home Loan Bank of Atlanta (FHLBank Atlanta) has been located in the city since 1971, but its roots extend back to 1932, when the U.S. Congress passed historic legislation to help the country recover from the Great Depression.

Today, more than seven decades after Congress created the Federal Home Loan Bank System, the Atlanta bank is privately owned by close to 1,200 shareholder-member financial institutions throughout Alabama, Florida, Georgia, Maryland, North Carolina, South Carolina, Virginia, and the District of Columbia.

With more than $115 billion in assets, the Bank's mission is to provide financial products and expertise to increase homeownership, affordable rental housing, and employment, and to promote community and economic development. The Bank accomplishes this by raising funds in financial markets, then distributing them to member savings institutions, credit unions, banks and insurance companies as a reliable source of long-term, low-cost funding to finance home mortgages and small business loans.

But FHLBank Atlanta is more than just a banker's bank; it is also a community builder. The Bank provides targeted housing and economic development grants, down-payment assistance for first-time homebuyers, and reduced-rate loans for specific community development programs. These programs create jobs, provide services, build low-income housing, give rise to neighborhood enhancements, and make communities better places for people to live.

These results were what Congress envisioned in 1932 when it passed the Federal Home Loan Bank Act to help Americans battle back from the debilitating effects of the Great Depression. The act was one of many enacted during the Depression to provide consumers with more access

to credit and help lenders provide more credit within their communities. Its prime purpose was to support the basic element of the country's economic well-being: homeownership.

The federal act created 12 district banks, each serving a specific region of the country. According to then-President Herbert Hoover, the system was "not a government (entity) but a cooperative institution between the building and loan associations, the savings banks and other home-loan agencies."

The law came out at a time when the thrift industry's Savings and Loan Associations, which had been created to offer home mortgages in local communities, were hard-hit by the Depression. They needed a system to safely provide mortgage credit, and that's what the Federal Home Loan Bank Act provided.

The creation of the regional system allowed local thrift institutions to offer longer-term mortgages, in both good and bad times, without depending entirely on local deposits. The system also led to the creation of the 30-year, fixed-rate mortgage, which today remains the most popular instrument for home financing.

> ## The Bank's Affordable Housing Program has helped fill the affordable housing gap in the region by providing millions of dollars in grants and enabling tens of thousands of families to have a place to call home.

Not only was the system a success, FHLBank Atlanta, then located in Winston-Salem, North Carolina, led the way. It became the first of the 12 regional banks to show a profit — and in its first full year of operation. The bank moved its headquarters twice before 1971, when it relocated to Atlanta, which had become a thriving financial and transportation hub for the South.

During its history, the FHLBank Atlanta has remained in a position to grow, as well as promote growth in the communities it serves. In 1989, the Financial Institutions Reform and Recovery Enforcement Act opened membership in the FHLBank system to commercial banks and credit

unions, and in 1998, the Gramm-Leach-Bliley Act updated the capital structure and governance of the FHLBanks and broadened its mission and purpose. These acts led to even more growth for the Atlanta financial institution.

Today, FHLBank Atlanta is the largest in the system in terms of assets and the volume of loans to members. The bank's funding products and services enable its member institutions to better handle their daily liquidity and cash-management activities, giving them the ability to fund more mortgages and loans.

In addition, the Bank's Affordable Housing Program has helped fill the affordable housing gap in the region by providing millions of dollars in grants and enabling tens of thousands of families to have a place to call home. The Bank also offers a range of community-investment services that support economic development and capacity building for nonprofits and community developers.

The bank's almost 300 Atlanta-based employees also do their part to help the community. They volunteer thousands of hours and donate thousands of dollars each year to charitable and civic organizations.

As for the future, FHLBank Atlanta will become increasingly important to the industry and the economic development of the communities it serves. As the financial services industry becomes more competitive, community banks will need access to alternative funding sources. The Bank remains committed to helping its member institutions access those funds and to building stronger communities.

LeasePlan USA

Headquartered in Alpharetta, Georgia, LeasePlan USA is one of the largest vehicle leasing companies in the United States. In 1983, the company began operating as a wholly owned subsidiary of LeasePlan Corporation, an innovative global leader in vehicle leasing and fleet management solutions. In 2000, LeasePlan USA acquired Consolidated Services Corporation, combining the global leader in leasing with a pioneer of fleet management

services. Today LeasePlan USA manages more than 400,000 vehicles for a broad range of clients including large multi-national corporations, nationally based companies as well as regional and local companies.

LeasePlan is the principal brand of its parent company LeasePlan Corporation. The company currently manages more than 1.25 million cars and trucks around the world and employs more than 7,200 people in 27 countries. The company's reach includes 21 countries in Europe, where it is the industry leader, as well as Australia, New Zealand, India, South Africa, Brazil and the United States.

LeasePlan Corporation has more than 40 years of fleet management industry experience. The company's goal is to build its leadership presence in all global markets and keep opportunities for expansion in new countries under constant review. By focusing on its clients and leveraging its global expertise, LeasePlan is committed to building its leadership presence in the industry through a highly proactive service approach.

LeasePlan's core business is leasing and managing vehicles. The company offers a broad range of leasing options and fleet management services to meet each client's changing needs. The company offers its clients comprehensive maintenance and repair management programs, accident management programs, risk management programs and fuel management programs. Services such as emergency roadside service, glass repair/replacement, license and title management and others can also be utilized for total fleet management.

In addition to leasing and managing company vehicles, LeasePlan USA also operates a Truck Division that provides individually tailored financial programs to some of the most recognized global and Fortune 1000 companies. LeasePlan's Truck Division experts work within each client's logistical framework to provide leasing services that achieve specific tax, accounting and cash flow objectives, as well as asset management. Examples of the types of assets LeasePlan's Truck Division leases include fork-lifts, material handling equipment, corporate aircraft and tractor-trailers. LeasePlan's goal is to establish long-term relationships with its clients by offering quality service and expertise, competitive rates and custom leasing services.

LeasePlan's Truck Division also has an arm dedicated to the health care industry. LeasePlan Healthcare offers health care companies the opportunity to keep up with changing technology by providing flexible leasing options to maintain state-of-the-art health care facilities.

LeasePlan's dedication to providing its clients with the highest level of proactive service is one of its distinct advantages. The company operates a live Customer Contact Center that is available 24 hours a day, every day, year round. Driver calls are handled by certified repair technicians with an average of 20 years of automotive repair/fleet maintenance experience. LeasePlan's Maintenance and Repair Management department has been awarded the ASE Blue Seal of Excellence for seven consecutive years, providing drivers the highest level of service by the most qualified technicians. In addition, LeasePlan is the only fleet management company to receive I-CAR (Inter-Industry Conference on Auto Collision Repair) Gold Class Certification for 11 consecutive years. The Gold Class Certification program was created to recognize businesses within the automotive collision industry committed to quality and excellence through training. Continued recognition by industry organizations such as these reaffirms LeasePlan's dedication to providing its clients with unmatched quality service and exemplifies the company's mission of proactive client satisfaction.

To further strengthen the company's commitment to service excellence, LeasePlan provides its clients with a dedicated account executive who averages 10 years experience in the automotive industry. LeasePlan's Client Relations Department is designed to meet and exceed the specialized needs of its clients. The department is divided into teams based on the geographic location of the clients they service. If clients are unable to reach their dedicated account executive, they are immediately routed to another knowledgeable team member assigned to their location who can provide them with assistance.

LeasePlan also distinguishes itself by being the only fleet leasing company in the United States that is registered by Underwriter Laboratories Inc. to the International Organization for Standardization ISO 9000 Series Standards for Quality. ISO refers to a series of documents that provide international guidelines on quality management and quality system elements. By providing quality management, LeasePlan fulfills its customer's quality requirements and applicable regulatory requirements while aiming to enhance customer satisfaction and achieve continual improvement of its performance in pursuit of these objectives.

The global fleet management industry is highly competitive, and LeasePlan is dedicated to offering its clients a proactive approach to new product development and improved services. Continued enhancements and developments in communication equipment, information systems, e-business, credit cards, EDI billing, client services and quality standards are required to stay competitive in today's marketplace.

LeasePlan strategically invests in technology to help streamline the tasks of fleet management. Its commitment to becoming a technological leader began more than a decade ago in 1993, when the company incorporated electronic data interchange and implemented a state-of-the-art imaging system enabling its staff to operate and handle transactions electronically in a paperless environment.

LeasePlan has always been committed to providing new technology to better serve their clients. As the Internet became increasingly more important to the way

LeasePlan customers conducted business, LeasePlan launched ePlan, a business-to-business Internet-based client management solution. ePlan allows customers to access vital imaged documents in real-time and easily download them into PDF format if necessary. The program also gives customers the ability to perform daily tasks more efficiently, such as ordering, selling, managing drivers and gathering reports by accessing the information via the Internet. Customers no longer have to maintain stacks of paperwork for each vehicle, saving them storage costs and further modernizing the documentation process.

LeasePlan also offers eTrack, a fleet management service that allows clients to maintain their own database of information allowing downloads of data from multiple vendors. Clients can enter all vehicle inventory and operating data for their fleet into the software and quickly generate reports for further analysis. Clients can access information such as inventory profiles, operating cost comparisons, replacement summaries, mile-per-gallon summaries, preventative maintenance alerts and other specific reports.

LeasePlan continues to stay at the forefront of innovative solutions. When vehicles come off lease, LeasePlan analyzes each sale and attempts to market each vehicle to ensure the greatest net return. To improve vehicle resale values, LeasePlan now offers its customers reDrive, the only completely automated online employee sales program powered by the technology of Driveitaway. Clients are able to post vehicles coming off lease on a Web site where their employees can then purchase the vehicles at below retail prices. The process is automated and completely upstream, saving clients valuable time and money. In addition, LeasePlan is introducing a new door-to-door delivery service in metropolitan areas across the United States to limit drivers' downtime when receiving new vehicles. This allows LeasePlan customers to remain concentrated on their core business.

As a leader and innovator in the fleet management industry, LeasePlan is committed to exceeding client expectations by ensuring the highest quality service and expertise. With more than 40 years of experience and a strong global presence, the company has made its place as a leader in the fleet management industry. LeasePlan is dedicated to providing its clients with proactive service and the latest technology to better serve their business.

National Financial Services Group

Many people are intimidated by financial planning, whether they're setting up a college fund, buying life insurance, or investing in the stock market. Yet, thousands of people across the country rely on National Financial Services Group to help them build a better future.

The reason boils down to one simple fact: trust. As a financial service firm that specializes in all areas of personal, business, and estate planning strategies, the company has a century-old track record of actively listening to its clients' needs, then developing realistic strategies to help them reach their financial goals. Its long history of success has earned both the company and its employees a national reputation not only as financial experts, but also as people who truly care about helping others balance many of life's challenges, no matter how small.

The company specializes in small business markets, ranging from physician practices and law firms to entertainers. Some of its associates have been with National for more than 40 years, strong evidence that National

Financial Services Group is an employer of choice and has never swayed from its original mission of helping people secure their financial future.

LEADERS IN ACTION

National Financial Services Group was originally launched as a traditional life insurance agency by John T. Moody and Walter C. Dobbins in 1896. Back then, the company was called the Atlanta Agency of National Life of Vermont. Built on a foundation of knowledge and integrity, its leadership changed in 1903 when George M. Hope purchased Moody's interest in the business and served as its general agent.

By 1925, the agency had become very successful, booking 7,339 policies throughout Georgia. Three years later, Dobbins passed away, then Hope the following year. Their sons ran the agency until 1945, when the two general agencies of The National Life of Vermont — headed by Dobbins' son and the firm of Haas & Dodd merged — naming Harold T. Dillon, Sr. as its general agent. The firm was now called The Dillon Agency.

For nearly 20 years under Dillon's leadership, the company flourished. Its sales force grew from three full-time agents to more than 100 throughout Georgia, Florida, and South Carolina. The Dillon Agency quickly evolved into a business model for the life insurance industry.

Dillon became well known for his expertise in agency administration and agent recruitment and training. During the next decade, sales continued to soar. In 1963, the agency's 110 representatives set an all-time record by writing $76.5 million of insurance policies, far exceeding the sales of any of the other estimated 1,200 life insurance companies at that time.

By the time Dillon retired in 1964 as a consultant for National Life of Vermont, he was the first insurance salesman to be elected a member of National Life's board of directors and was a life member of the industry's Million Dollar Round Table. Likewise, he had served as chair of Georgia State College's advisory council in 1962. The school established the Harold T. Dillon Fund in 1964 to promote life insurance education and scholarship aid for life insurance students.

Dillon, perhaps the industry's greatest general agent, passed away in 1978. His values and ideas still propel the company as it moves forward into the next century.

GROWTH OPPORTUNITIES

In 2000, James L. Cook, Jr., ChFC, CFS, took over the reigns and began growing the company into a full service financial planning firm that supports a variety of in-house specialists. Among its many associates are certified public accountants, certified financial planners, chartered financial analysts, chartered financial consultants, chartered life underwriters and certified fund specialists. Unlike some of its competitors, National Financial Services Group delivers one of the broadest ranges of financial products and services in the industry, creating a one-stop shop for clients.

It was renamed National Financial Services Group in 2000 to better reflect its diverse menu of service offerings representing more than 200 insurance companies.

In addition, associates who are Registered Representatives of Equity Services, Inc., offer securities from a number of investment management companies that manage more than $13 billion in assets and represent more than 6,000 mutual funds.

Under the umbrella of National Life Group are subsidiaries such as Equity Services, Inc., that offer a comprehensive range of stocks, bonds, mutual funds, variable life insurance, asset accumulation, and retirement planning products. Others include American Guaranty & Trust, which provides complete personal trust and custody services, National Retirement Plan Advisors, offering comprehensive retirement plan services, The Sentinel Family of Funds, one of the country's oldest mutual fund families, and ESI Financial Advisers, which offers fee-based asset management programs from some of the best money managers around the world.

The companies work as a team, creating solutions that are as different as their clients' needs. Some people need help defining their investment goals, exploring ways to save on taxes or protecting their family against financial loss due to death or illness. Others may have questions like, "Will they outlive their retirement income?" or "How much liability insurance should their business have?" Whatever the scenario, the company's professional staff helps people build and protect their financial resources.

The process begins by asking the right questions and gathering facts. As clients lead the way, the company develops strategies to help them reach financial independence. Client meetings are also scheduled on a regular basis to help people review their plans or make any necessary adjustments to adapt to changing lifestyles without getting off track.

With help from superior technology, the complexities of financial services are also simplified for clients, further demonstrating National Financial Services Group's commitment to providing excellent client service. The end result is that clients become more confident in their ability to invest wisely and chart a successful financial future.

At National Financial Services Group, Managing Money Matters℠ since 1896, clients always come first, a corporate philosophy that supports the firm's mantra, "When our clients win — we win." As a result, the firm will continue in its efforts to earn people's trust and business for another 100 years while helping to shape the country's financial industry.

TLS Service Bureau

Founded in 1997, Atlanta-based TLS Intelligence, is a leading national provider of corporate and domestic intelligence services, with an emphasis on detecting, preventing and prosecuting white-collar crime.

In six short years, TLS retained more than 500 clients by helping them lower the cost and risk of doing business. TLS was ranked one of the city's 50 fastest-growing private companies by the *Atlanta Business Chronicle*, and one of the 500 fastest-growing companies in the nation by *Inc.* magazine.

"TLS has achieved phenomenal growth not through mergers and acquisitions, but instead the old-fashioned way, by developing and retaining one satisfied customer at a time," says co-founder Todd A. DeStefano.

Since 1997, TLS expanded from three employees to more than 60 and added offices throughout the United States and the world. According to DeStefano, two prime reasons account for the company's impressive growth.

Thomas L. Santamorena, Founder, President, CEO

The first is that DeStefano and co-founder Thomas L. Santamorena brought strong, diverse backgrounds to TLS. DeStefano has a law degree and a breadth of insurance experience, while Santamorena has a background in retail loss prevention. The two met while working as fraud investigators for a large insurance carrier.

> **TLS was ranked one of the city's 50 fastest-growing private companies by the *Atlanta Business Chronicle*, and one of the 500 fastest-growing companies in the nation by *Inc.* magazine.**

The second reason for the company's impressive growth is the strong need for the services that TLS provides. White-collar crime in the United States, says DeStefano, "is an increasingly expensive burden on the U.S. economy, which takes money out of the pockets of all citizens. With an estimated annual cost of more than $200 billion per year and growing, it creates a hidden tax of $2,500 per family each year on the costs of goods and services."

"TLS is committed to combating this fraud and to saving our clients the losses sustained by these criminal acts," DeStefano says. "This ultimately leads to cost savings for each and every U.S. family that purchases insurance or pays inflated prices on goods and services due to providers' corporate markets, as well as in insurance and risk manincreased cost of doing business."

TLS works to reduce the cost of white-collar crime to businesses and to the general public. The company provides solutions for clients in the legal, financial and corporate markets, as well as insurance and risk management. TLS assists banking and corporate clients in identifying and eliminating all types of white-collar crime, including fraud and embezzlement.

In addition, a variety of business market changes, emerging global markets, expanding information technology and increasing competition have created a more uncertain atmosphere in which commerce is conducted. These changes have increased the need for companies to do business with strangers, and expanded business for TLS.

TLS offers consulting services including non-financial due diligence, litigation support, asset tracing, pre-acquisition due diligence and investigations of fraud and intellectual property infringements. Other specialties include pre-employment screening, drug testing and surveillance services. The importance these latter services has been highlighted by high-profile scandals at a number of large corporations.

"A thorough employee background screening is just as important as any other type of business due diligence, especially if the employee will be handling money and credit cards or dealing with the public," DeStefano says. "Businesses should conduct a background check or full screen before they hire a person. One bad hire can create millions of dollars of damages due to lost reputation, as well as compensatory and punitive damages."

Insurance services offered by TLS include field adjusting; underwriting, claim and fraud investigations; auditing; claim profiling and surveillance. TLS also stresses the importance of conducting background checks on vendors and other businesses before entering into a relationship.

TLS offers consulting services including non-financial due diligence, litigation support, asset tracing, pre-acquisition due diligence and investigations of fraud and intellectual property infringements.

"When a business offers it services through a vendor or sub-contractor, those individuals are viewed by the public as an extension of your company," DeStefano says. "So when it's time to enter into an agreement with a vendor, know where your vendors have been. Or perhaps it's time to merge with another business. How thoroughly will you check into the background of their people? Using TLS Intelligence's investigative due diligence service prevents a business from losing potentially large sums of money, and sometimes, from completely collapsing. It is as important to investigate vendors and potential employees as you would any other business."

Among its successes, TLS saved a law firm a large sum of money by determining that a company it was about to acquire was only a shell, and its principal planned to take the money and run. In another instance, a TLS investigation showed that a man suing his former

TLS works to reduce the cost of white-collar crime to businesses and to the general public. The company provides solutions for clients in the legal, financial and corporate markets, as well as insurance and risk management.

employer for a catastrophic injury was working and not confined to a wheelchair, as he had claimed. The man was arrested for insurance fraud.

The segment in which TLS works is a fast-growing one. However, TLS does not believe that all investigative companies are created equal. DeStefano and Santamorena, while working as insurance investigators, became dissatisfied with the quality of firms providing services similar to those they currently offer. They decided their firm would maintain the highest professional standards.

The TLS staff is carefully selected and trained to work in partnership with company clients. They are responsible for conducting complete, professional investigations within time frames designed to give clients the right information at the right time, so that they can make effective management decisions. In addition, TLS offers bilingual investigators.

As well as fighting white-collar crime, TLS believes in being a good corporate citizen. Company personnel are active members of numerous organizations, including Rotary Club, The United Way and the St. Vincent DePaul Society, as well as many others.

The company is active in developing community service projects that address many of today's critical issues, including children at risk, poverty, hunger, the environment, illiteracy and violence.

"We also support programs for youth, educational opportunities and international exchanges for students, teachers and other professionals, plus vocational and career development," says DeStefano.

Colonial Bank

From supporting high-rise communities to engaging in relationships with elderly citizens, Colonial Bank's involvement in Atlanta has become a shining example of the financial giant's personal touch in communities of the six states where the company has bank offices.

In Atlanta, the headquarters of the Georgia region, Colonial is involved in several major projects, including two high-rise communities. Also, Colonial has financed a continuing care community in Stone Mountain, where the company also has an office.

Colonial Bank, Member FDIC and an Equal Housing Lender, is committed to partnerships with the people, the places and the pastimes that make Atlanta great, and it supports Atlanta through projects that make the city a wonderful place to live. Colonial Bank has actively invested in the continued growth of Atlanta through its financing of several major parks and communities where residents live, work and play.

The success story of Colonial Bank is a people story, rooted soundly in the professionalism and dedication of the Colonial Bank employee group. Colonial employees are local people who know the financial needs of their customers and their communities. Colonial has concentrated on expanding from its base in Alabama into four of the five fastest-growing states in the nation: Georgia, Florida, Nevada, and Texas.

Since Colonial's beginning in 1981, more than 60 community banks have been acquired and merged into Colonial Bank, integrating them into a structure that contributes to Colonial's community banking philosophy. Colonial Bank, a subsidiary of The Colonial BancGroup, Inc., opened the first Georgia office in 1995 and now has more than 20 locations throughout the state.

A board of directors made up of business men and women from Atlanta, Columbus, and Macon supports the regional management team, which allows better responsiveness to customer and community needs.

Colonial Bank believes that supporting local businesses, organizations and charities fosters a genuine trust and accountability between the citizens of Atlanta and the employees of the bank. Colonial is a corporate partner with the United Way, donating thousands of dollars to the yearly campaign. Employees and customers alike can purchase a "shamrock" to assist the Muscular Dystrophy Association in raising money during the annual MDA's Shamrock Project. The bank has also supported the Jewish Federation of Children and Family Services, an agency that offers adoption and welfare-to-work services that coach unemployed residents in job-seeking skills. Several area elementary schools benefit from the personalized attention of Colonial Bank employees who donate their time to meet with the PTA, judge a spelling bee, or teach English as a second language (ESOL) classes.

The Colonial BancGroup, Inc. is a multibillion-dollar bank holding company, headquartered in Montgomery, Alabama, with full-service offices in Georgia, Alabama, Florida, Nevada, Tennessee, and Texas. Colonial is a super-community bank committed to providing customers with helpful attention and services they deserve. "Our success has come from one-on-one dealings with folks in Atlanta," says Georgia CEO Walter Parrent. "I think what people appreciate in this city more than anything else is being treated as individuals."

Palmer & Cay, Inc.

Georgia-based Palmer & Cay, Inc. represents the knowledge, the vision and the future of risk management services, exemplifying the next wave of risk management capabilities and expertise for the 21st century.

Established in Savannah in 1868, Palmer & Cay built its reputation as a premier brokerage organization by combining excellent client service with expert advice. Through the years, the firm has never wavered in pursuit of its goal: to be the industry's most respected firm. Thus it provides the best array of creative solutions available to meet clients' broad-based risk management needs. These needs include those associated with a client's property and casualty insurance; their people, including employee benefits, compensation, human resources and retirement plans; and their assets, including investments. With a national presence of some 1,000 employee associates and 38 offices operating in 22 states and the District of Columbia, Palmer & Cay is the nation's second-largest privately owned brokerage firm.

The secret behind the firm's unsurpassed success in offering risk management services is Palmer & Cay's distinctive way of conducting business. Palmer & Cay upholds a longstanding commitment to

do the right thing and to always act in its clients' best interests. The firm promotes a culture based on a genuine concern, respect and courtesy shown for the individual, whether it is a client, an employee, a partner or a supplier. To achieve superior results, Palmer & Cay stays focused on its primary objectives: satisfying client needs and serving its employees. The firm continually works to understand its constituents' needs and wants — and to always exceed expectations on both counts.

The result of this culture is Palmer & Cay's consistent ability to attract the best and the brightest professionals in their respective fields. The single-company approach to solving client issues and problems ensures that Palmer & Cay's clients have access to the firm's most-qualified specialists to deal with their particular needs, regardless of location.

Palmer & Cay's services include risk management consulting, insurance brokerage, risk control, reinsurance, surety bonds, executive liability, captive insurance structuring, health and welfare benefits plan consulting and brokerage, retirement plan and investment consulting, executive compensation consulting and human resource consulting. In addition to technical expertise in a number of disciplines, Palmer & Cay also specializes in key industry sectors including aviation, marine, design and engineering, construction, equine, private equity and health care. The firm's trade affiliations include the Worldwide Broker Network, Independent Insurance Agents of America, Inc., Council of Insurance Agents & Brokers and the International Broker Network.

Guided by the mission to be the best firm in the industry, but not necessarily the largest, Palmer & Cay continues to draw accolades for the creative solutions its staff develops for clients, for the professional and ethical way in which business is conducted, and for the firm's vision of how the risk management business must be managed. Palmer & Cay truly embodies the next wave of the risk management industry.

"Atlanta is the undisputed business capital of the South. At the Terry College, we've been working hard to weave our faculty and programs into the fabric of Georgia's business community, and Atlanta is at the heart of that strategy."

P. George Benson, Dean
Terry College of Business
The University of Georgia

EDUCATION

Atlanta area educational institutions and the businesses that support them provide citizens of all ages with learning opportunities in diverse subjects and environments.

Terry College of Business

The University of Georgia's Terry College of Business has made quite a splash with Atlanta's business community since plunging back into the metro area after a four-decade absence. Coinciding with its growing presence in Atlanta's financial district, the college's inner workings have also been reorganized to better reflect a school whose purpose is to develop leaders for the world's private enterprise system. To this end, the Terry College stresses leadership assessment and development opportunities throughout its curriculum. Its flexible graduate programs, taught at an attractive corporate campus, are supplemented by talks from prominent executives and complemented by interactive technology that's convenient for full-time executives.

The Terry College was founded in 1912, when the University of Georgia (UGA) authorized a School of Commerce to begin instruction, making it the oldest business school in the South and one of the oldest in the nation. By 1947 the school, renamed the College of Business Administration, had assumed responsibility for the Evening School of Commerce in Atlanta. After eight years, the state's Board of Regents decided to spin off the school into a new and separate university that became Georgia State University.

Over the decades, the college's reputation for faculty excellence continued to grow and the school underwent a metamorphosis. In 1977 the college created one of the first five schools of accounting in the nation, and in 1979 it became the first college in the nation to offer a master's degree in marketing research. Atlanta's boom as a technology, hospitality and transportation center during the 1980s and 1990s spawned an influx of workers, capital, resources and economic growth — and the demand for business graduates surged dramatically. The college was

ready for the challenge, and Dean Al Niemi, who envisioned that UGA would someday be back in business in Atlanta, began a major capital campaign to increase the college's endowment, growing it from $3.5 to $32.5 million. Today it stands at more than $60 million. Niemi also created the Georgia Economic Outlook luncheon in Atlanta, an important harbinger that the college intended to become visible again in the capital of the South.

In 1991 the college was renamed the C. Herman and Mary Virginia Terry College of Business to honor two distinguished benefactors whose support made possible a number of endowed faculty chairs, research fellowships and scholarships. In 1995 a fire seriously damaged Brooks Hall, home to the Terry College in Athens since 1927, but the building was beautifully restored and reopened in 1997. At the same time, alumni, friends and the corporate community fully funded a new high-tech classroom building in Athens named for UGA graduate Charles S. Sanford Jr. and his wife,

Mary McRitchie Sanford. Coinciding with the expansion in facilities, enrollment grew as well. As recently as 2001, the college's undergraduate program was one of the five largest in the country.

With all this growth and renewal, it was clearly time for the Terry College to take a giant leap forward, and new Terry College of Business Dean P. George Benson would be the visionary who would provide the means for the college to do so. After Benson arrived from Rutgers University in 1998, he took stock of the college. Although it was "a very good meat and potatoes business school," it offered little in the way of executive education for middle- and senior-level managers and no revenue-generating degree programs in off-campus locations. Benson created a leadership council consisting of faculty, staff and students and charged them with developing a strategic plan that would propel Terry into prominence as an institution that helps educate and train the business leaders of the present and future. The council reached a consensus on the purpose for the Terry College — to develop leaders for the world's private enterprise system. An in-depth analysis of Terry's current state of affairs identified opportunities for future success and the college developed a set of strategic goals and laid out the infrastructure necessary to achieve them.

To support the college's purpose, the Institute for Leadership Advancement was established to help students and executives enhance their leadership potential and skills. Programs include individualized leadership development for undergraduate and MBA students and an executive leadership program teaching personal leadership for managers.

The plan also stressed the urgent need for Terry College to return to Atlanta's corporate community — to

The Arch is the University of Georgia's most distinctive landmark.

college offers nine distinct degree programs in Athens and Atlanta. They are the Bachelor of Business Administration (BBA) in Athens; the BBA in Gwinnett; the Master of Business Administration (MBA) in Athens; the Evening MBA in Gwinnett; the Executive MBA in Buckhead; the IBM-Terry MBA, designed for management consultants of IBM Business Consulting Services; the Master of Accountancy in Athens; the Master of Marketing Research in Athens, for professionals in market intelligence and marketing research; the Master of Internet Technology in Gwinnett, for students who desire a balanced curriculum between technology and e-commerce management; and the Ph.D. in Business Administration in Athens, awarded in eight disciplines.

The Terry College will excel in the 21st century by continuing to focus on creating leaders for an economy in which dominance in knowledge will create competitive advantages for firms. In addition to being the business school of choice for undergraduate and MBA students interested in becoming leaders, the college will continue to provide lifelong learning opportunities for its alumni and other members of the business community in Atlanta and across the state.

integrate Terry programs more closely with Atlanta's corporate culture. In March 2000 the Terry College launched a breakfast speaker series — "Terry Third Thursday" — at the university's new Alumni Center in Atlanta's Buckhead district. It was Terry's first new program in Atlanta since the 1950s and it paved the way for several more important Atlanta programs: an Evening MBA and undergraduate BBA program at the Gwinnett University Center, an Executive MBA program in Buckhead, and the twice-a-year Directors' College designed for current and prospective corporate directors.

The University of Georgia and the Terry College of Business were back in Atlanta with significant programs. And by teaming up with corporate partners in Atlanta and around the state to offer residencies, internships, training, consulting and a monthly speaker series, these public-private partnerships are having the desired effect of weaving Terry into the fabric of the business community and the business community into the college's classrooms.

Today, through an effort to manage enrollment and offer optimal class size, the Terry College has a student body of about 3,000 and a faculty numbering 150. The

TERRY COLLEGE OF BUSINESS RANKINGS

PUBLICATION	RANK
U.S. News & World Report	
Undergraduate Program	27
Insurance	4
Real Estate	5
Management Information Systems	16
Accounting	18
Graduate Program (MBA)	42
Management Information Systems	17
Accounting (MAcc)	29
Financial Times of London	
Public MBA Program	22
Forbes	
Public MBA Return on Investment	20
Computerworld	
Techno MBA	Top 25
Entrepreneur	
Top Entrepreneurial Colleges	Top 50

Kennesaw State University

Betty L. Siegel, president of KSU since 1981, was the first woman to head a University System of Georgia institution. During her tenure, the university has evolved from a four-year college with an enrollment of 4,000 students and 15 baccalaureate-degree programs to its current university status, with nearly 18,000 students and more than 55 undergraduate and graduate degree programs.

A distinctive commitment to student success represents one of the most important ways in which Kennesaw State University (KSU) has achieved its current position as a standout public university in the University System of Georgia. Chartered in 1963, Kennesaw State serves as a valuable resource for the densely populated and rapidly developing northwest region of metropolitan Atlanta by providing award-winning degree programs, community outreach and cultural opportunities. KSU implements institutional improvements to meet the needs of its increasingly diverse and constantly changing learning community. The dedication of KSU's more than 1,100 full-time faculty and staff members, an annual operating budget of more than $127 million, state-of-the-art campus housing, myriad student organizations and activities, a vibrant athletic program and numerous outreach and research centers, not to mention nearly 18,000 students, all contribute to KSU's stature as a progressive and exemplary educational institution respected for its excellence and leadership in teaching, service and applied research.

While Kennesaw State shares numerous qualities with the other institutions within the University System of Georgia that make it a desirable place for students to pursue a higher education, it also possesses a unique and independent identity that enhances this appeal. At the core of its success lies KSU's dedication to effective teaching and learning, buoyed by both service and applied research that strengthen teaching while addressing public interests. KSU's faculty, staff and administrators strive to provide an environment conducive to high-quality academic preparation, critical thinking, global and multicultural perspectives, effective communication and interpersonal skills, leadership development, social responsibility and lifelong learning.

All of KSU's undergraduate students take part in a comprehensive general education program designed to promote global and connected learning in the liberal arts tradition. Students select from a wide range of baccalaureate degree programs, including majors in the arts, humanities, social sciences, mathematics, natural sciences, business, education, computing and information systems, and nursing. In addition, KSU's expanding selection of professional master's degrees includes education, business, public administration, professional writing and nursing.

The increasing number of students choosing to enroll at KSU includes young adults who enroll as freshmen or undergraduate transfers and an equally large number of older adults who look to the university at different stages in their lives for undergraduate or graduate study. While most students are classified as commuters, often pursuing their academic goals while balancing job, family and civic responsibilities, a growing number reside in state-of-the-art, on-campus housing. Evening and weekend programs accommodate experienced professionals seeking academic advancement. In addition, a broad range of programs, services and activities are offered outside the classroom to enrich campus life and enhance students' success and personal development.

The Burruss Building houses the Michael J. Coles College of Business, which includes the second largest Executive MBA program in the nation. The Executive MBA recently received two top-10 ratings from *BusinessWeek*, in e-business and teamwork categories.

Significant and growing numbers of international and minority students enroll at KSU every year, including more than 1,500 international students representing 129 countries.

KSU's expanding selection of professional master's degrees includes education, business, public administration, professional writing and nursing.

Recognizing this expanding diversity in its student population, KSU sponsors an assortment of programs designed to promote a multicultural and international

educational environment, from its Distinguished Diversity Lecture Series to study abroad opportunities in more than 10 different foreign countries. KSU's Institute for Global Initiatives, established in 2003, has a broad, university-wide mission to spearhead KSU's international efforts. In addition to the study abroad programs, the institute provides academic programs and services to internationalize the curriculum and expand international opportunities for faculty, staff and students and the greater community.

Along with its vast array of educational offerings, KSU upholds a longstanding commitment to public service. The university plays a vital role in promoting and supporting regional interests in the visual, performing and cultural arts. KSU also supports and participates in an extensive number of continuing education programs, nationally recognized lectures and conferences, collaboratives with public schools, partnerships with business and governmental agencies, international initiatives, service institutions and outreach centers.

One such outreach center, the university's RTM Institute for Leadership, Ethics & Character, promotes ethical leadership through education, training, research and programs focused on principles of ethical conduct, character development, stewardship, service and community engagement. Receiving a $1 million endowment in January 2003 from RTM Restaurant Group allowed the institute to sharpen its focus on leadership, stewardship, ethics and character development both on campus and throughout the community.

The American Council on Education recently selected KSU as one of eight institutions in the country for a study entitled "Global Learning for All," which will focus on good practices in promoting international student success. In addition, the university's dedication to fostering excellence in public service brought it recognition from the American Association of State Colleges and Universities as one of the

nation's top publicly engaged universities in its study, "Stepping Forward as Stewards of Place." KSU was also named one of 12 founding institutions in a project called "Foundations of Excellence in the First Year of College," by Dr. John Gardner and the Policy Center on the First-Year College Experience. For this study KSU is conducting a comprehensive analysis of its own policies and programs related to the freshman experience.

Determined to strengthen international relationships while also fostering the advancement of northwestern Georgia, including the area of metropolitan Atlanta where it is located, KSU takes pride in its well-deserved reputation as a meritorious educational institution. More than four decades of commitment to the success of its students, as well as to promoting and effecting positive changes on both local and global scales, have earned Kennesaw State University recognition as a progressive institute of higher learning characterized by excellence in service, applied research, teaching and learning.

(Left)
KSU's award-winning campus grounds provide a beautiful environment for students to study and learn. Projects such as the Campus Green highlight Kennesaw State's transformation from a commuter college to a comprehensive residential university.

(Right)
Large-scale building projects such as Kennesaw Hall have changed the face of Kennesaw State in recent years. Other facilities, including student housing and a classroom/convocation center, are designed to serve the needs of KSU's growing student population as well as the surrounding community.

Kids 'R' Kids International Inc.

The childcare industry has definitely been enhanced as local entrepreneurs, Pat and Janice Vinson, rose to the challenge to provide the best facility, best equipment and the best educational programs.

The Kids 'R' Kids International corporate headquarters is located in Duluth, Georgia. Kids 'R' Kids International was established in 1985 by Patrick and Janice Vinson, who are presently active in the company as President and Vice-President.

Their past experience of operating a school began in 1961. In bringing with them their 44 years of experience in childcare and reaching out with the technological advances of today, Pat and Janice have created a concept that is unique and on the leading edge of the child care industry. As seasoned educators who saw the need for consistent excellence in education, the Vinsons have developed their vision into a dynamic, rapidly growing franchise. Today, Kids 'R' Kids franchises exist in over 110 schools throughout Georgia, Florida, Kansas, Kentucky, Mississippi, Nevada, North Carolina, Ohio, South Carolina, Tennessee, Texas and Puerto Rico. This proven system of excellence is continuing to rapidly expand into other states as well.

Each Kids 'R' Kids School of Quality Learning is independently owned and operated. The average school size is 13,000 square feet, with approximately 250 students and 45 teachers. Each Kids 'R' Kids has quality educational programs for age groups from infants to 12 years old.

SCHOOLS OF QUALITY LEARNING: The Kids 'R' Kids foundation is built around developing partnerships between parents and teachers. This mutual relationship

offers the strongest education and optimum care for every child. Kids 'R' Kids exceeds the minimum standards of childcare by providing established educational concepts and programs where children can grow from infancy through their elementary school years.

Each franchise is planned with the children in mind. Teachers are trained to recognize and meet the needs of each child, using highly developed curriculum tailored to each age group. Learning is divided into units, focusing on a different theme each month. Complementary activities and corresponding reading concepts accompany each unit. Plenty of outside time, field trips, cultural activities, before-and-after school care, and summer camp round out the experience.

Parents discover and appreciate all the enhancements that Kids 'R' Kids has made to the childcare and education industry. Gone are the enclosing structures, the limited hours, and communication loss between school and parent. Instead, a tour through any participating Kids 'R' Kids franchise reveals tempered glass walls, activities galore, closed-circuit cameras with viewing monitors in the lobby, and telephones and daily communication for parent-teacher.

The Vinsons have introduced technological changes to enhance the parent's peace of mind and open communication. Parents and grandparents need not be onsite to observe their child's school time experiences. Secure

Internet access viewing allows families the opportunity to see firsthand their child in his or her learning environment. The site is secure and can be accessed only with the parent's password.

TRAINING: Kids 'R' Kids International, Inc. supports each school and its teaching staff through ongoing early childhood training. In order to offer more within the school and the classroom, each staff member is trained in all areas of early childhood development.

Each Kids 'R' Kids School of Quality Learning is encouraged to exceed the minimum standards in order to encompass the latest research in early childhood development. Kids 'R' Kids believes the more one knows about a child and their developmental stages, the better that person can reach out and attend to all the needs of the child. Each member of the corporate training department is experienced in teaching adults. The entire educational course work that is taught has been approved through each state's childcare service regulatory department.

QUALITY ASSURANCE: Kids 'R' Kids International, Inc. supports the excellence of each School of Quality Learning through biannual inspections. The Quality Assurance staff is trained to inspect each school for health and safety by examining; building and bus maintenance, family and staff records, state and local inspections, menu selections and food preparation, outdoor play equipment and play areas, classroom cleanliness and appropriate arrangement, and the overall well-being of children in the school. Once an inspection report has been generated, each school has a short and specific time frame to correct any non-compliance sightings. This service is extended to all Kids 'R' Kids Schools of Quality Learning, which assists them in maintaining the excellence that every family deserves.

CURRICULUM: Kids 'R' Kids International, Inc. is proud of the curriculum developed and produced. The writers in the corporate Curriculum Department are professional educators with more than 75 years of combined classroom instruction, administrative positions and curriculum development. The Kids 'R' Kids Curriculum is predicated on the National Association for the Education of Young Children (NAEYC) curriculum standards and embraces the concepts of the renowned psychologist, Jean Piaget. By providing an educational environment, Kids 'R' Kids is able to implement learning objectives established by national teacher organizations. In doing so, Kids 'R' Kids

offers theme-based lesson plans, which integrate "real life" subject matter, order and sequence. Kids 'R' Kids also provides engaging and enriching activities that are developmentally appropriate for learning centers and play-based classrooms.

The Kids 'R' Kids theme-based Seasonal Core Curricula was developed for children two through five years and additional themed units, as well as school-aged activity calendars, are written for children kindergarten through fifth grade for use in after school care, winter breaks and summer camp.

Kids 'R' Kids recommends The Active Learning Series, along with sign language for infants, one and two-year-old children. This well-known curriculum for preschool children has proven to be successful in the classroom and at home. We have found that our youngest students are even learning through care giving times as their teachers are implementing classroom activities with attentive love.

All activities reinforce newly learned concepts for children of any age and are encouraged by the staff members at Kids 'R' Kids Schools of Quality Learning.

FRANCHISE OPPORTUNITY: Kids 'R' Kids International offers an exciting, innovative approach to educating children, and generates business opportunities for entrepreneurs interested in joining the franchise team. Kids 'R' Kids International points the way to the education of the future, offering a new way to enhance our most valuable resources — our children and our community.

We Hold The Future®

Greenforest/McCalep Christian Academic Center

The Greenforest Community Baptist Church was incorporated on June 5, 1959, in Decatur, Georgia. The church, itself, experienced initial popularity, but with a large congregational population decrease in the mid 1970s, the Atlanta Baptist Association reduced it to an 18-month partial mission status. It was the Reverend George O. McCalep, Jr., who, being called in 1979 to serve as pastor of Greenforest, successfully transitioned the church from its partial mission status to a full congregationally owned and autonomously governed Baptist church.

Not only did he accomplish this for the church, but he also managed to multiply its congregational count from 25 to over 6,000 members. Because of his broad biblically based theological ministry, the church is spiritually appealing to its members, including new converts, seasoned converts and restored converts who might have been wounded by previous church experiences. Moreover, through his passionate and faithful teachings of Biblical church growth

and stewardship, the annual church budget has swelled from $13,000 in 1979 to over $5 million. Today the total combined Greenforest ministry budgets come to an impressive $11 million.

Thanks to Pastor McCalep's ingenuity, Greenforest was also able to establish and develop its Greenforest/McCalep Christian Academic Center (GMCAC) in 1989, opening it to students of all races, colors, national and ethnic origins; granting them all rights, privilege and access to all programs and activities. GMCAC welcomes every child of families who, in line with the philosophy of the church, are willing and eager to learn how to build a biblical community of

loving relationships — students are daily taught to devoutly love, follow and model Christ. GMCAC integrates academic excellence with Christian principles, a love for God, knowledge of His saving power, a sense of self-worth, a respect for others and a strong sense of African-American heritage.

GMCAC competently educates young people via its "Early Learning Center," the largest pre-school learning center in the southeastern region of the United States, which teaches ages six weeks to four years old. The "Academy Program" offers a strong spiritual and academic program for children in Kindergarten through the 12th grade. The academy also offers multiple electives, college preparatory and advanced placement courses to all middle school and high school students. All programs teach every attending child to confront life's challenges and pursue their aspirations through "Academic Excellence — God's Way" by offering daily Bible classes, devotion time and weekly chapel visits, as well as before school and after school student care, summer enrichment programs and summer advantage academic programs. GMCAC's curriculum serves students academically, spiritually and culturally — emphasizing African-American history — using methods of positive reinforcement and recognition programming; through a safe and controlled environment.

GMCAC is a member of and is fully accredited by the Association of Christian Schools International (ACSI), which is recognized and approved by the State of Georgia. The academy is also accredited by the Southern Association of Colleges and Schools (SACS), and is a member of the National Institute of Independent Schools. In addition, GMCAC is in the top four to 10 percent of all schools nationally, as determined by the standardized test of basic skills.

The academy has attained this recognition by bringing experience and professionalism to educate students on a Biblical foundation with Christian values. It is because of Greenforest/McCalep Christian Academic Center faculty's careful planning and thorough preparation that it is the spiritual, academic and social development-augmenting venue that benefits the overall well-being of its diverse student body.

Mercer University

Mercer University is committed to academic excellence in creating intellectual and moral capital for a new generation. With 7,300 students on campuses in Atlanta and Macon as well as three regional academic centers across the state, Mercer has 10 schools and colleges and is one of the most diverse institutions of its size in the country.

Mercer was founded in Penfield, Georgia, in 1833, under the leadership of prominent Georgia Baptist leader Jesse Mercer. The university originally had planned to move to Atlanta, but instead went to Macon in 1871 when the city offered it a substantial gift of land.

It was another 88 years before Mercer established an Atlanta program. The opportunity came in 1959 when Southern College of Pharmacy, located in downtown Atlanta, merged with the university. Thirteen years later, Atlanta Baptist College, which had opened in 1968 on a 300-acre campus in northeast Atlanta, asked to merge with Mercer, strengthening the Atlanta connection.

Today, the university's Cecil B. Day Graduate and Professional Campus in Atlanta is home to six of Mercer's 10 schools and colleges.

One of the shining jewels in the Mercer crown of academic excellence is the Southern School of Pharmacy, one of only two pharmacy schools in Georgia. Offering the doctor of pharmacy degree and the university's only doctor of philosophy degree, the school is also a center for grant-funded research and clinical studies.

The oldest nursing program in the state, Georgia Baptist College of Nursing merged with Mercer in 2001. The college

works with some 50 major hospitals and health care organizations in Atlanta and is the only nursing program in the Southeast to require three years of clinical training.

Students gather outside the Georgia Baptist College of Nursing of Mercer University.

The McAfee School of Theology brings Jesse Mercer's founding vision of providing students with a classical and theological education full circle as it partners with the Georgia Baptist Convention and Cooperative Baptist Fellowship. Students enter McAfee to prepare themselves for the ministry of the next century.

As the largest private preparer of teachers in Georgia, the Tift College of Education is also the university's largest school. The Atlanta program offers both master's and specialist's degrees in education as well as initial teacher certification.

In the Eugene W. Stetson School of Business and Economics, business students may pursue the executive master of business administration degree, master of business administration degree or complete their bachelor of business administration degree.

The College of Continuing and Professional Studies offers a master of science in community counseling degree, which prepares students to work with people in health care, business, educational and residential environments.

The Stetson School of Business and Economics in Atlanta offers evening degree programs.

From its beginnings more than 170 years ago, Mercer has grown into a premier academic institution. *U.S. News & World Report* consistently names Mercer as one of the leading universities in the South and *The Princeton Review* has listed Mercer among "The Best Colleges in North America." Mercer's presence in Atlanta will continue to grow and share its heritage of excellence for years to come.

Morehouse School of Medicine

There's an infectious spirit at the Morehouse School of Medicine (MSM), beginning with the school's motto — "the small medical school with outrageous ambition" — coined by the institution's president.

It's evidenced by the school's commitment to recruit and train future physicians, biomedical scientists and public health professionals to continue in MSM's mission to meet the primary health care needs of the underserved.

It also can be found in the school's marked growth since its humble beginnings in 1975, as a two-year school called The School of Medicine at Morehouse College.

The vision of Dr. Louis W. Sullivan, the medical school's first dean and president, has continued with successive leaders — including MSM's current president, Dr. James R. Gavin III — and through its vast milestones. For one, the Morehouse School of Medicine is proud to be home to the nation's only primary care center — the National Center for Primary Care, headed by the 16th U.S. Surgeon General Dr. David Satcher.

Today some 2000 applicants from around Georgia, the nation and the world compete for the approximately 50 slots open to incoming M.D. students at the four-year institution. In the beginning, students were able to receive

> ## Morehouse School of Medicine may be small in size, but its ambition is most certainly "outrageous."

two years of basic sciences at the medical school, after which they transferred to other institutions to complete their clinical training. In 1981 the institution became separate from Morehouse College and authorization was given to expand to four years. Two years later, MSM became part of the Atlanta University Center, the largest consortium of historically black institutions of higher learning.

Spring of 1985 saw the degree of Medical Doctor (M.D.) conferred on the school's graduating class, and by

1990, MSM provided all the necessary clinical training of its students.

The Morehouse School of Medicine offers a variety of accredited residency programs, including Preventive Medicine, Internal Medicine, Obstetrics and Gynecology, Surgery, and Graduate Medical Education. In 2001 a

pediatrics residency program was initiated. MSM's reputation as a top research institution (ahead of nearly one-third of all medical schools in the United States), along with its unique mission of recruiting minority students to administer care among the nation's underserved attracts the attention of hopeful candidates from around the world. Eighty-four percent of M.D. graduates from the Morehouse School of Medicine practice in medically underserved areas, and 68 percent of M.D. alumni work in primary-care disciplines. Compared to national averages (about 25 percent of physicians train in primary care disciplines nationally), Morehouse School of Medicine graduates emerge well ahead of the pack.

Of the nation's 125 medical schools, the Morehouse School of Medicine is a standout example of excellence. It is no small thing to combine the muscle of academia with the heart of service. Together MSM's flexed muscle and beating heart impact people here in Atlanta and in ever-widening circles, populations the world over. Morehouse School of Medicine may be small in size, but its ambition is most certainly "outrageous." That ambition, when applied to its mission of working to eliminate health disparities, leaves a remarkable legacy.

"The Coca-Cola Company exists to benefit and refresh everyone it touches." *The Coca-Cola Company Promise*

The Coca-Cola Company and Coca-Cola Enterprises Inc.

Atlanta has been the home of Printpack since its founding in 1956, and together we have grown to become an international presence. Atlanta offers our associates an outstanding quality of life and provides a wonderful place to raise our families. Our involvement in this community and commitment to its citizenship continues to run deep, and we are proud to be a part of its great heritage.

Dennis Love, President & CEO
Printpack Inc.

MANUFACTURING & DISTRIBUTION

In addition to producing exceptional goods for individuals and industry, regional manufacturing and distribution companies provide employment for residents.

The Coca-Cola Company and Coca-Cola Enterprises Inc.

THE COCA-COLA COMPANY

For generations, The Coca-Cola Company has been associated with fun, refreshment, good times and value. From "Delicious and Refreshing," to "Things Go Better with Coke," "You Can't Beat the Feeling" and "Real," the world's most famous soft drink is "Always Coca-Cola."

Today Coca-Cola is one of the world's most-respected brands and the company behind it is one of the most renowned worldwide. Its advertising slogans are the stuff of pop culture, its logo is readily recognized and its successes have rendered it a leader in the global business community.

But this icon of international business — the world's leading manufacturer, marketer and distributor of nonalcoholic beverage concentrates and syrups — actually began quite inauspiciously.

The Coca-Cola legend started with Dr. John Stith Pemberton, an Atlanta pharmacist who stirred up a caramel-colored syrup in a three-legged copper kettle that stood unassumingly in his back yard. On May 8, 1886, Pemberton felt that he had finally perfected the formula for his delicious concoction, so he carried the syrup down to the local soda fountain at Jacobs' Pharmacy. There it was mixed with carbonated water and sold, chilled, of course, to its first consumers. For a mere 5 cents a glass, Atlantans could enjoy what would one day become the world's most popular soft drink.

This new beverage needed a name. It was Pemberton's partner and bookkeeper, Frank M. Robinson, who suggested "Coca-Cola." The two Cs created a memorable alliteration for the public's effortless recollection, and it was perfect for advertising. Once Robinson created the celebrated trademark and penned the words Coca-Cola in the now-famous Spencerian script, the first inviting advertisement appeared in *The Atlanta Journal* on May 29, 1886.

As Pemberton's health began to fail, another pharmacist stepped in to add another dimension to the legend that was being built. Asa G. Candler recognized Coca-Cola's potential immediately. He began acquiring Pemberton's interests in the business venture until a total investment of $2,300 bestowed him sole ownership of the company in 1891. The next year Candler gathered his business

partners together and founded a new Georgia corporation to further promote the brand.

A candy store owner named Joseph A. Biedenharn decided in 1894 to broaden the distribution and sales of Coca-Cola, which until then had been sold only as a fountain drink. He installed bottling equipment in the back of his Vicksburg, Mississippi, store and sold cases of the beverage up and down the Mississippi River.

Although Biedenharn may have been the first official bottler and distributor of the new refreshment, it was two men from Chattanooga, Tennessee, who acquired the rights to bottle and sell Coca-Cola nationwide. The dynamic network of bottlers that they started still operates today and whole-heartedly sustains the entire Coca-Cola family of brands.

As time progressed, the company continued to evolve and saw many changes in management, beginning with Ernest Woodruff, who bought the company in 1919 for $25 million. Woodruff reincorporated The Coca-Cola Company in Delaware and for the first time, publicly sold 500,000 shares of common stock at $40 per share. His son, Robert Woodruff, led the company through six decades of progress. It was during Robert Woodruff's tenure that the company transformed into a truly global business.

In 1981 Roberto C. Goizueta became chairman and chief executive officer. The Cuban-born leader had begun his career as a chemist in Havana, but he rose to the company's highest ranks and effectively boosted its market value from $4 billion to $145 billion. He also established The Coca-Cola Foundation, which supports programs in higher education; classroom teaching and learning; and international education. Its programs also support scholarships for aspiring students; encourage and motivate young people to stay in school; and foster cultural understanding.

In 2004 the board of directors named E. Neville Isdell, an Irish citizen and veteran of the Coca-Cola system, as the chief executive officer and the 12th chairman of the board.

Today the company produces more than 300 brands that are distributed in more than 200 countries. Its products include carbonated soft drinks, juices and juice drinks, bottled water, sports drinks, milk- and soy-based drinks, tea and coffee. The company has 5,000 employees in Atlanta. About 77 percent of the company's operating income excluding corporate was generated outside the United States in 2002.

The company's promise is to benefit and refresh everyone it touches. And to that end, The Coca-Cola Company not only provides beverages and refreshment, it also gives back to the communities where it does business.

From education to the environment, community development, and health and wellness, The Coca-Cola Company offers its philanthropic support in many ways throughout the world. For example, it builds schools and trains teachers in many parts of the world; supports rainwater harvesting in regions that routinely suffer from droughts; promotes literacy programs in the United States; provides scholarships for higher education; offers AIDS-related health benefits in Africa; and it supports the Olympic Games, the Special Olympics, the Federation of Internationale de Football and many other sports programs at the grass roots level.

While its business and philanthropy span the world, The Coca-Cola Company will always be a part of Americana. People of all ages reminisce about sipping Coca-Cola at the drugstore counter, listening to the strains of "I'd like to buy the world a Coke ...," watching the Coca-Cola Polar Bear ads on television, or tasting their first Vanilla Coke. Some collect Coca-Cola memorabilia; others simply enjoy the nostalgia — a nostalgia that is built like the company — on fun, refreshment, good times and value.

COCA-COLA ENTERPRISES INC.

When Coca-Cola was first invented by pharmacist John Pemberton in 1886, a customer would have to visit a drugstore soda fountain to enjoy it. Today it's available worldwide, not by accident, but through the hard work and dedication of Coca-Cola Enterprises and other Coca-Cola bottlers.

Founded in 1986 Coca-Cola Enterprises is the world's largest, yet local, marketer, producer and distributor of products of The Coca-Cola Company. The brands of The Coca-Cola Company represent some of the most popular beverage brands in the

world. Coca-Cola Enterprises produces and sells approximately 24 percent of The Coca-Cola Company's worldwide volume, distributing products in bottles, cans and fountain containers.

Coca-Cola Enterprises is in the nonalcoholic beverage business; its product line extends beyond traditional carbonated soft drink categories to beverages such as still and sparkling waters, juices, isotonics, coffee- and milk-based drinks, and teas.

The process begins when concentrate made by The Coca-Cola Company is sold to the bottlers, and shipped

to production facilities. Suppliers also deliver sweetener, concentrate and purified water (essential to making products that taste exactly the same no matter where they are produced). These ingredients are mixed together to make simple syrup.

Empty cans or bottles are then rinsed and sent to the fillers, which can produce up to 2,000 beverages per minute. Cans are closed with a seamer that attaches a metal lid, and a code date is printed on each can for quality assurance. Glass and plastic bottles are capped and dated.

Finished beverages are packaged into containers for distribution and spend a brief time in a warehouse until employees deliver them to be stocked in a distinctive Coca-Cola vending machine or on a store's shelf.

The first bottling franchise began operations in 1899, serving parts of Tennessee and other nearby locations under the ownership of Benjamin F. Thomas and James F. Johnston, grandfather of Coca-Cola Enterprises' former chairman and chief executive officer, Summerfield K. Johnston, Jr.

The Coca-Cola bottling system continued to work as independent, local businesses until the early 1980s when the bottling franchises began to consolidate. In 1986 The Coca-Cola Company merged some of its company-owned operations with two other large ownership groups to form Coca-Cola Enterprises. Another merger took place in 1991 between Coca-Cola Enterprises and the Johnston Coca-Cola Bottling Group, Inc., accelerating the consolidation process.

For over 100 years, Coca-Cola bottlers throughout their territories have supported their communities as they helped to develop the Coca-Cola brand and build their businesses. These links remain vital to Coca-Cola Enterprises' business today, as demonstrated by its strong commitment to maintaining a local focus to the business and serving its communities and customers with a passion.

Employees are involved in a broad array of community activities and initiatives, helping every day to improve education, to aid local charities and to strengthen neighborhoods and cities. In activities as varied as supporting

the National PTA, Junior Diabetes Research Foundation and Camp Coca-Cola, to helping local youth sports leagues, and serving important roles in local chambers of commerce, Coca-Cola Enterprises employees work to help those around them, with a special focus on supporting positive youth development and physical activity.

This approach extends throughout Coca-Cola Enterprises' business as well. Employees play a major role in customer success by increasing the presence of Coca-Cola at the neighborhood level. In community schools, the company strives to be responsive and respectful of the rights of parents, teachers and students to choose the beverages for their schools. They encourage positive choices about

physical activity, and health and wellness through their program, "Your Power to Choose... Fitness Health Fun."

In every market, in every town, in every Coca-Cola Enterprises facility, there are similar examples of employees' efforts to help and improve the local areas they serve. It is a foundation of their business, which is why Coca-Cola Enterprises' philosophy of "Close to Home" is essential to the company's success.

The company operates in parts of 46 states in the United States; all 10 provinces in Canada; and portions of Europe including Belgium, continental France, Great Britain, Luxembourg, Monaco and the Netherlands. Coca-Cola Enterprises' franchise territories encompass a population of almost 400 million people and serve thousands of communities.

Coca-Cola Enterprises employs approximately 74,000 people who operate more than 450 facilities, 55,000 vehicles, and 2.5 million vending machines, beverage dispensers and coolers. Coca-Cola Enterprises initially offered its stock to the public on November 21, 1986, and is listed on the New York Stock Exchange under the symbol "CCE."

Through their vast contributions and prominent presence — in beverage supply and beyond — The Coca-Cola Company and Coca-Cola Enterprises provide enjoyment and benefit for people all over the world. Indeed, both companies' appeal to consumers parallels their business environments in that they are the refreshing outcomes of ardent work, assiduous care and attention to quality.

IDI

Distribution.

It's a weighty word, and not particularly exciting — unless it is being used to explain one of the most critical factors of successful supply-and-demand management over the past 25 years. And playing an important role in this management of supply and demand is a dynamic network of big-box distribution centers and warehouse facilities. They serve as the heart of commerce, pumping products across the country where they're needed and when they're needed.

Consumers typically don't see this network of big buildings behind the check-out stand or the "submit order" prompt. But Henry D. "Greg" Gregory, Jr., sees that network. In fact, he helped to develop it.

Gregory, president and chief executive officer, also is the founder of IDI, which consistently is named among the top industrial real estate developers in the United States. The company is headquartered in Atlanta, with regional offices in northeast Atlanta, Chicago, Cincinnati, Dallas, Fort Lauderdale, Los Angeles and Memphis. By the date of this publication, the company had developed throughout the United States some 100 million square feet of Class A industrial real estate space valued at more than $3.3 billion.

Gregory founded IDI at his kitchen table in 1989 with help from several colleagues who, like him, had left an international firm that couldn't clear the recessionary hurdles of the late 1980s. To get started, Gregory sought

and won financial support from his strong contacts in the business; it was a matter of being in the right place at the right time, with the right idea and the right people.

"In those early years, when a lot of other developers were retracting, we were expanding," Gregory says. "In hindsight, that recession actually helped us. We were able to get market share that probably would have been more difficult for us to obtain in a robust market."

Today, thanks to IDI's enduring financial strength, manufacturing and distribution firms have access to a number of development options to best meet their real estate needs:

• **Inventory properties,** often referred to as speculative buildings, provide immediate lease occupancy in IDI business parks located in prime distribution hubs throughout the United States. These hubs include Memphis, Tennessee, also known as "America's Distribution Center;" Southern California, which includes the critical Inland Empire region; and other logistically strategic U.S. metropolitan markets.

• Custom **build-to-suit properties** provide long-term leasing opportunities or direct client ownership. They are developed under a negotiated or competitive-bid basis, and on a site controlled by the client or on an IDI-owned parcel of land.

• A **for-fee development** option offered through IDI's National Fee Development (NFD) group is designed to allow clients as much or as little participation in the development process as they like. NFD becomes an extension of the client's own internal real estate and/or logistics resources, and client interests are represented through an open-book development process from start to finish.

• An impressive list of clients — including The Home Depot, Sony, Circuit City, UPS Supply Chain Solutions, AmerisourceBergen, Wal-Mart, Office Depot and Hewlett-Packard — have repeatedly

(Right)
IDI's national development services include building, leasing, managing, and selling and buying industrial real estate.
Photo by John Benoist

(Below left)
IDI maintains a sufficient level of inventory space and land estates throughout the United States to respond to market demands based on economic conditions per region. This allows the company to meet single- or multiple-property needs, coast-to-coast and with as an aggressive development plan as necessary.
Photo by Cotten Alston

(Below right)
Looking after the grounds is only a small part of the job for IDI Services Group real estate managers, who also help manage a property's financial landscape on the owner's behalf.
Photo by John Benoist

partnered with IDI for comprehensive, **multi-facility development** solutions. These companies' national programs mirror industry trends of consolidation and increased efficiency through an optimal number of strategically placed warehouse and distribution facilities.

• Through a joint venture with The Rockefeller Group, IDI provides clients with the expertise and capabilities to take advantage of significant savings in operations by locating in buildings and/or parks designated as **Foreign Trade Zones (FTZs)**. These FTZs provide enormous economic advantages, particularly in terms of duty savings and inventory cost reductions.

In addition to these real estate development services, IDI provides comprehensive property management, leasing and construction management services through its subsidiary, **IDI Services Group** (IDISG). IDISG manages property for IDI tenants, and for tenants of third-party owners such as pension funds and insurance companies. "We create value in the properties we handle through aggressive hands-on management, high tenant-retention rates and attention to detail," said Tim Gunter, IDI's senior vice president and chief operating officer. Though it's one of the largest industrial real estate managers in the United States, IDISG still provides personal client service, local market knowledge and meticulous attention to detail, taking a building-by-building operating business approach and employing aggressive leasing tactics that achieve dramatic results in a short time.

A merchant developer, IDI continues to be the nation's leading seller of industrial real estate to the investment community. This status is maintained by a continued focus on not only the needs of the industrial real estate user, but also the needs of the industry investor. By matching investors to the right product, IDI has, since 1989, closed more than $2.3 billion in sales transactions, representing an impressive list of clients such as CIGNA Investment Management, Lend Lease Real Estate Investments, J.P.

Morgan, L&B Realty Advisors, Sun Life Assurance Co. of Canada, TIAA-CREF, and TA Associates Realty Advisors. These companies recognize at least one common denominator in all IDI developments, whether located in South Florida or in northern Illinois.

That's quality.

"We have two clients: the users who occupy the building and the investor who buys it," Gregory says. "It's easy to satisfy both of those important sectors at the same time if you build and maintain quality projects."

A certain segment of the real estate industry understands that with opportunities in commerce come responsibilities to communities. Throughout its seven U.S. district offices and from its headquarters in Atlanta, IDI and its employees provide funding and/or time to a number of civic, cultural and environmental organizations.

Nationally, IDI continues its strongest support for The Trust for Public Land. This is the only national nonprofit organization working exclusively to help conserve land for recreation and spiritual nourishment and to improve the health and quality of life of U.S. communities. Greg Gregory, president and CEO of IDI, is chairman of the National Real Estate Advisory Council and a member of the Georgia Advisory Council. IDI employees also assist TPL-Atlanta with critical special projects.

Henry D. "Greg" Gregory, Jr.
Photo by Don Rank

Through Senior Vice President and Chief Financial Officer David Birdwell, IDI contributes significant time and funding to The Study Hall at Emmaus House in Atlanta. The organization is designed to help the seriously at-risk child grow out of a negative atmosphere and into a world of knowledge and self-esteem.

The Atlanta Opera also has received significant funding from IDI. The Opera strives to present opera productions of the highest standards possible while fostering education about the art form and encouraging its growth. Gregory also serves as a board member of The Atlanta Opera.

In 2002, Gregory was named a trustee to The Woodruff Arts Center, for which he has served as co-chairman of the real estate committee several years prior. One of the most dynamic visual and performing arts centers in the South, The Woodruff Arts Center encompasses the Alliance Theatre Company, High Museum of Art, Atlanta College of Art, 14th Street Playhouse and the Atlanta Symphony Orchestra.

As one of the nation's leading developers of industrial real estate, IDI prides itself on developing Class A distribution and warehouse facilities in prime distribution markets throughout the United States.
Photo by Dave Brown

Printpack Inc.

With almost 50 years of experience in the manufacture of packaging materials, today's Printpack Inc. upholds its longtime commitment to "packaging better ideas™" for its customers. Owned and operated by members of the Love family, Printpack remains guided by old-fashioned family values, believing that cooperation, honesty and an active adherence to high ethical standards result in the highest-quality packaging products for its customers. Printpack's tradition of holding fast to such principles while incorporating the latest technological innovations into its packaging solutions has yielded an unbeatable combination for its customers.

During a 30-year career with the company he founded, Erskine Love grew Printpack from a one-man operation to a packaging industry leader.

This tradition began with Printpack's founder, J. Erskine Love Jr. who started the company in 1956 as a one-man operation with a single piece of equipment — a used cellophane bag machine. Mr. Love created a successful business in a remarkably short time through his personal determination and his focus on segments of the growing food industry. During its first decade in business Printpack grew rapidly to include 150 associates, and shortly thereafter the company began its westward expansion, constructing its first facility outside of Atlanta in 1969 in Grand Prairie, Texas. That same year growth by acquisition became a crucial tactic for Printpack's expansion, beginning with Southeastern

Printpack's wide array of products helps protect and market many of the world's leading branded consumer goods.

Packaging, Inc. During the following two decades, this trend continued via acquisitions of Standard Packaging, Sigmadyne Corporation, and Daniels Packaging.

Printpack's rapid pace of innovating and expanding its operations continued throughout the 1970s and 1980s, starting with the development of extrusion laminating in 1970, which subsequently became a key process for Printpack and its products. High fidelity graphics requiring the utmost precision also developed rapidly during this period, fueled by strong customer demand. By the time it celebrated its 20th anniversary in 1976, Printpack was a substantial business with over $35 million in sales and almost 500 associates at its two sites in Atlanta and Texas.

Printpack's continued technological innovations resulted in a growing reputation and increased recognition among its customers and in its industry. For example Printpack was a 1984 double winner in the Flexible Packaging Association's Annual Packaging Competition. Though by no means the first award Printpack had received, this dual recognition solidified even further its preeminence in the flexible packaging industry. The following year *Business Atlanta* named Printpack's founder and president, Erskine Love, as the Atlanta 100 Entrepreneur of the Year — an especially distinctive honor as the recipient is chosen by his or her peers from the city's largest private companies.

In 1987 Erskine Love died suddenly of a heart attack. His oldest son, Dennis, who had worked for the family company since 1978, was named the company's new president.

Under the leadership of Dennis Love the company maintained its commitment to excellence as it moved into the 1990s and ultimately the 21st century. In 1993 Printpack went international through its acquisition of Flexpack in the United Kingdom. Three years later Printpack became one of America's two largest flexible packaging companies through its purchase of the packaging operations of the James River Paper Company. With this acquisition Printpack became a force in rigid packaging as well, an expertise that has continued to grow and flourish. Today with more than 4,000 talented associates at 20 production sites and more than $1 billion in annual sales, Printpack serves the diverse packaging needs of the world's largest consumer product companies.

The company's newest product designs provide consumer-friendly features that incorporate the convenience, high-impact graphics and superior barrier properties that today's market demands. Printpack's stand-up pouch with a resealable zipper has proven useful in applications such as pet food, cereal, snacks, and lawn and garden. Another innovative package looks like paper but is actually a highly protective plastic film structure — an ideal design for packages that need great protection but depend on a paper-like appearance for brand identification. In the rigid packaging arena Printpack has led the way in making glass and metal packages obsolete, offering safer and more convenient plastic containers as an alternative for products like applesauce, fruit, pudding and baby food. These packaging solutions represent just a few examples from the impressive list of Printpack's latest inventive concepts.

Along with pioneering new ideas in packaging Printpack upholds the highest standards in manufacturing capabilities and in analytical services. Recognizing the importance of continuously reinvesting in manufacturing facilities and equipment, the company offers customers the latest in flexible packaging technology, including blown monolayer and coextruded films, cast coextruded films, flexographic and rotogravure printing, extrusion and adhesive laminations, holography and much, much more. Printpack's Analytical Services Laboratory offers customers package breakdowns, shelf life testing, odor/aroma characterization, and physical testing, while its expert staff can assist with regulatory issues such as FDA compliance, analytical testing, methods validation, and data sheets.

In addition to its dedication to its customers, Printpack is committed to the preservation of the environment and to the manufacture of environmentally responsible products. Thus the company employs a staff of environmental professionals, including an environmental coordinator at each Printpack manufacturing facility responsible for policy compliance and regulatory reporting. Environmental initiatives include programs dedicated to internal recycling, toxic substance reduction and solvent recovery, all of which minimize the potential for both onsite and offsite contamination.

Complementing its commitment to the environment outside its doors, Printpack nurtures a company-wide environment in which trust, respect, continual learning and teamwork are highly valued, believing that such an environment fosters innovation and promotes continuous process improvements, which in turn benefit the customer. The company recognizes that the knowledge, dedication and expertise of its associates make its success possible and therefore offers a wide variety of ways for associates to improve their skills, including company-paid tuition plans, scholarship awards, internal training and development programs, and local computerized learning centers in each of its plants. Such dedication to progress gives both Printpack and its customers a competitive advantage in the marketplace.

As Printpack associates look to the future, they continue to be inspired by the words of company founder, Erskine Love, *"Be willing to encourage and accept change, to experiment, to explore the unknown, to take risks and, above all, seek excellence in everything you do."*

Atlanta has been the home of Printpack Inc. since its founding in 1956.

Printpack's multiple manufacturing facilities in the United States, the United Kingdom and Mexico produce millions of consumer packages every day.

Lockheed Martin Aeronautics Company Marietta, Georgia

Lockheed Martin Aeronautics Company (called LM Aero) is an industry leader in the design, development, systems integration, production, and support of advanced military aircraft. Customers include the armed forces of the United States and allied countries around the world.

The company's Marietta facility has been in operation under the Lockheed or Lockheed Martin name since January 1951. Current production programs include the C-130J Hercules airlifter and the F/A-22 Raptor air dominance fighter.

The Marietta plant, one of Lockheed Martin Aeronautics Company's three facilities, is also where development work is underway on two major upgrades of the C-5 Galaxy strategic transport, as well as where modification and sustainment programs for the P-3 Orion and S-3 Viking maritime patrol and carrier-based multimission aircraft are coordinated. Lockheed Martin is teamed with Alenia Aeronautica of Italy on the C-27J Spartan medium airlifter, and that work is also based in Marietta.

The facility was built during World War II for the production of B-29 bombers. Since reopening what is now called Air Force Plant 6, employees have built more than 3,250 advanced aircraft and modified nearly 7,500.

During that time, the Marietta plant has made business commitments with Georgia firms totaling more than $4 billion.

LM Aero also strives to make an impact on the communities where those employees live and work. The company promotes volunteerism, provides financial support, and donates other resources to support nonprofit organizations throughout the Atlanta area.

The future of the Marietta plant is positive.

The F/A-22, the world's most advanced fighter, is now completing testing and is meeting all of its technical goals. More than $200 million has been invested in specialized facilities in Marietta to build the stealthy F/A-22. The F/A-22 is the future of air warfare. It is also a significant part of the plant's future.

The C-130J, while externally similar to the more than 2,200 Hercules that have come out of the plant, is, in fact, a complete reinvention. The U.S. Air Force has a stated long-term requirement for additional C-130Js, so the Hercules will continue to be the plant's bread and butter for many years. A multi-year procurement contract for 40 C-130Js for the U.S. Air Force and 20 KC-130J tankers for the Marine Corps was signed in 2003.

The C-5, one of the world's largest aircraft, has approximately 80 percent of its useful life left, but its avionics, engines, and subsystems are becoming unreliable. To correct this, the Air Force has embarked on two efforts to enhance the C-5 fleet and replace its engines, and development work is centered in Marietta.

LM Aero has a solid business base and stable employment in Georgia. The Marietta plant is the only military aircraft start-to-finish assembly plant in the southeast, and it is among a few factories building aircraft of any type at all in the United States. The Marietta plant is truly a national resource.

Schweitzer-Mauduit International, Inc.

Schweitzer-Mauduit, with 2003 sales of $567 million, conducts business in 90 countries and employs 3,600 people worldwide producing premium specialty papers, and is the world's largest supplier of fine papers to the tobacco industry. Schweitzer-Mauduit's corporate headquarters, U.S. Business Unit and the research center are located in Alpharetta, Georgia. The international company maintains manufacturing facilities in North America at Ancram, New York; Lee, Massachusetts; Spotswood, New Jersey; and Winkler, Manitoba; in France at Quimperlé, Malaucéne, Saint-Girons and Spay; and in

Schweitzer family businesses were acquired by the Kimberly-Clark Corporation.

In 1995 Schweitzer-Mauduit became an independent public company in a tax-free spin-off by Kimberly-Clark Corporation to its shareholders. In 1998 Schweitzer-Mauduit acquired Companhia Industrial de Papel Pirahy — now Schweitzer-Mauduit do Brasil — a prestigious printing, writing and packaging paper producer and the largest supplier of tobacco-related papers in South America, and Ingefico, S.A. — now Papeteries de Saint-Girons — a tobacco-related and other papers and textile

(Left)
Paper roll from Spotswood, N.J. mill

(Center)
Final product (bobbins) used to produce cigarettes

(Right)
Robotic slitters producing bobbins from rolls

Santanésia, Brazil. It also has satellite sales offices in Paris, Rio de Janeiro and Hong Kong and an administrative office in Madrid. In addition, the company acquired a tobacco-related paper mill in Medan, Sumatra, Indonesia, in 2004.

Schweitzer-Mauduit started in 1906 as Peter J. Schweitzer, Inc., a family business based in New Jersey that imported cigarette papers from France. In 1922 the company acquired Papeteries de Malaucène, a paper manufacturer that has operated continuously since 1545 and ranks as a world leader in manufacturing perforated tipping and colored cigarette paper.

In 1940 Schweitzer acquired the Spotswood, New Jersey, mill, which today produces both cigarette paper and paper wraps for drinking straws.

A decade later Schweitzer acquired the Lee group of mills, in western Massachusetts. Additional acquisitions include Papeteries de Mauduit, located in Quimperlé, France, and currently the world's largest cigarette paper mill, and the Ancram mill, which dates back to 1743 and is now the heart of Schweitzer-Mauduit's reconstituted tobacco wrapper and binder business. In 1957 the

fiber pulp manufacturer in France. In 2003, at the Spay, France, mill, Schweitzer-Mauduit installed its third reconstituted tobacco leaf machine costing approximately $78 million and providing 33,000 metric tons per year of additional capacity.

Schweitzer-Mauduit International has grown significantly since its modest beginning as a family-owned company. The corporation manufactures cigarette paper, plug wrap paper, reconstituted tobacco leaf and tipping paper as tobacco industry products; and commercial and industrial products, such as lightweight printing papers, coated papers for packaging and labeling applications, business forms, base paper for furniture laminates, battery separator paper, wraps for drinking straws, filter papers and other specialized papers.

With its persistence for acquiring fine paper mills that supply the tobacco industry, the corporation has advanced rapidly — its tobacco-related papers account for 93 percent of Schweitzer-Mauduit's net sales — increasing its prominent position as a multi-faceted, diversified producer of premium papers for the tobacco industry.

"In our new 30-acre facility, my son and I are leading Allan Vigil Ford into the future of a growing and thriving South Metro Atlanta. Our loyal customers and hardworking, dedicated employees will continue to strengthen our business and our community."

Allan Vigil, President
Allan Vigil Ford

C-W-C is proud to be a part of Atlanta's prosperous community. For over 75 years, we have been providing classic office environments to our customers along with our strong customer service philosophy. The tremendous growth that the Atlanta community has experienced has contributed greatly to our position as the largest contract furniture dealership in the Atlanta market.

Paul Conley, President
C-W-C

"On behalf of our 300,000 associates, The Home Depot is delighted to be a part of Atlanta's growing community," said Bob Nardelli, Chairman, President and CEO of the company. "The continued support of the people of Atlanta, and the commitment of our associates, has helped The Home Depot to become not only the world's largest home improvement retailer but a leader in corporate citizenship and civic involvement."

Bob Nardelli, Chairman, President and CEO
The Home Depot

The JW Marriott Buckhead Hotel has enjoyed our close business allies with the Buckhead community. We are proud to be part of the most magnificent areas in the country to work, live and entertain!

Jeff Ford, General Manager
JW Marriott Hotel Buckhead Atlanta

MARKETPLACE

Retail establishments and the service, hospitality and recreation industries offer an impressive variety of choices for residents and visitors.

Allan Vigil Ford

Guided by president and owner M. Allan Vigil, Allan Vigil Ford has earned a much-deserved reputation for delivering a comfortable, hassle-free auto buying experience to each of its customers. In his recently opened spacious new location on Mt. Zion Boulevard in Morrow, Georgia, just south of Atlanta, he stocks an enormous selection of vehicles and has one of the largest service departments in the Southeast. The interior of the new facility is larger than four football fields, and there are parking spaces for more than 2,000 vehicles.

For customer comfort and convenience the dealership has multiple waiting rooms with digital televisions and Internet access connections, observation areas, a children's play area and the T-Bird Café — a 1950s style retro restaurant. Mr. Vigil's attention to customer comfort and satisfaction is immediately apparent to everyone who walks through the doors of the facility and has led to a high rate of satisfied repeat customers. Allan Vigil Ford has become not only Georgia's largest Ford dealer, but also one of the top 100 Ford dealerships in the country.

On the same dealership campus Mr. Vigil built a separate parts distribution facility to accommodate the dealership's brisk wholesale parts business, the best in the region. Next door is a free-standing, state-of-the-art collision center with 32 repair bays and five down-draft paint booths, easily the largest collision center in the southeast.

Allan Vigil, 2003

Allan Vigil began his automotive career with Ford Motor Company following his graduation from the University of Florida and military service. As a first lieutenant in the Army from 1967 to 1970, he served in Vietnam and was awarded a Bronze Star and an Army Commendation Medal for his actions.

After several years with Ford Motor Company he moved to the retail side of the automotive business, going to work as used car manager for the dealership in Jonesboro, Georgia, that he would later come to

own. He worked for a dealership in Macon, Georgia, for several years but was asked to return to Jonesboro to rescue what was then a failing business. Deeply in the red and with a poor reputation, the Jonesboro dealership was in great need of help.

> **...today's Allan Vigil Ford dealerships continue to enjoy a well-earned, first-rate reputation in the Atlanta metro area.**

To foster a successful business Mr. Vigil realized the critical nature of his leadership role and worked to increase sales volume while creating a high level of customer satisfaction. He put together a new management team, stressed taking care of the customer, and emphasized the importance of great service. Slowly the business began to recover and became a thriving local business. Several years later Mr. Vigil was offered the opportunity to buy out the owners. It now belongs to him, and he plans to keep it in the family.

With the help of a dedicated team of employees, all areas of the business have grown. According to Mr. Vigil "loyalty means something here." His service manager began as an 18-year-old working in the wash bay, and many employees have been with him a long time. Every effort is made to promote from within and much attention is given to in-house training and employee retention. During the grand opening ceremonies for the new facility, Mr. Vigil said that his employees were "first-class employees and deserved a first-class facility." It truly is a family atmosphere.

Allan Vigil Ford is one of the few dealerships in the area that is still a family business. Not only is it privately owned, but also Mr. Vigil's son, Mike, recently was named vice president. Having grown up in the dealership and worked in many different areas, Mike Vigil joined the dealership management full time following his graduation from Lynn University. He has proudly become part of the team committed to upholding the company's reputation for great service and customer satisfaction.

Throughout the years Allan Vigil Ford has been recognized with numerous professional honors, being a multiple recipient of Ford Motor Company's One Hundred Club, President's Award and Partners in Quality. Allan Vigil Ford's prestigious standing was recognized with Ford Motor Company's Triple Crown Award in 2002 and 2003. This award was given to only 17 of approximately 4,000 Ford dealers in the country. Allan Vigil Ford received the Hispanic Business Inc. 2002 Entrepreneur of the Year Award in the retail and finance category, and the Georgia Hispanic Chamber of Commerce named Mr. Vigil the businessman of the year in 2001. Mr. Vigil was a finalist for Ernst and Young's Entrepreneur of the Year Award in 2000 and was a recipient of the Electric Transportation Coalition's National and Local EV Hero Awards in 1999, among other awards and recognitions.

Continued success in the automotive business prompted Mr. Vigil to acquire an additional Ford franchise, Allan Vigil Ford Fayetteville, in February 2003. Mr. Vigil plans to keep the Fayetteville dealership at the present location and grow the business by creating the same customer satisfaction and loyalty enjoyed at the original Allan Vigil Ford. The Fayetteville location has an atmosphere of a true hometown Ford dealership.

Allan Vigil and Mike Vigil in front of a vintage Ford truck

In addition to his professional awards and recognitions, Mr. Vigil stands out as a community-minded entrepreneur involved in a wide array of civic activities. Recently appointed to the Board of Regents for the University System of Georgia, he is also a board member for Southern Regional Health System; on the board of directors of Community Capital Bank in Morrow, Georgia; and a board member of the Alliance of Ford Motor Company Minority Dealers; among his many other community and civic affiliations.

From the moment he took reins of Allan Vigil Ford, Mr. Vigil's sure-handed leadership and intelligent, customer- and community-oriented approach to creating a top-notch auto dealership have met with repeated success. By embracing the core values of focusing on customer service and satisfaction while staying ahead of the field in technological innovations, today's Allan Vigil Ford dealerships continue to enjoy a well-earned, first-rate reputation in the Atlanta metro area.

Allan Vigil Ford (new dealership completed 2003)

C-W-C

C-W-C's reputation for providing quality products and unparalleled service has remained its focus since it first opened its doors as a small furniture dealership back in 1929. As the company has grown through the years, expanding its products and services, it has correspondingly augmented its already sterling reputation. Today C-W-C continues to develop and enhance

all facets of its business, from furnishings and design to project management, providing each and every client with the unprecedented level of customer service that has characterized C-W-C for more than seven decades.

In 1929 James Wallace, John B. Courtenay and Harold G. Carithers opened a small showroom in the heart of downtown Atlanta that would one day become one of the Southeast's most prominent furniture dealerships. Throughout C-W-C's first 40 years each founder served as president and then as chairman of the board. Tremendous growth in these initial years led C-W-C to expand from a sales company to a sales/service company that offered design support services as well as office supplies and furniture.

C-W-C's first 40 years of success prompted the 1969 move into a much larger facility, still in the heart of downtown Atlanta, where it continued to grow. In 1975 C-W-C began a longstanding partnership with two leading office furniture manufacturers, Kimball Office Furniture and Herman Miller. The original innovator of the panel system, Herman Miller, allowed C-W-C to offer its easily

installed and reconfigured products. These products possess the highest residual value in the furniture industry and continually evolve as technology changes. Herman Miller also created and continues to set the industry standard in ergonomic seating, currently with its Aeron chair. Kimball Office Furniture led and continues to lead the industry in case goods and wood seating products. Such successful partnerships established a precedent that would lead to C-W-C's current representation of more than 300 of the finest contract furniture manufacturers in the industry.

The 80s and 90s brought with them enormous changes as C-W-C worked to adapt to constant shifts in its customers' requirements as well as to a marketplace saturated with mergers and acquisitions. In 1988 the company moved into its much-needed larger showroom space, a 178,000-square-foot facility in northern Atlanta. C-W-C expanded into the Macon marketplace during the early 90s by establishing its first branch office, which would allow the company to efficiently reach other markets within the state. In 1995 C-W-C's management responded to the climate of acquisitions and mergers by agreeing to allow U.S. Office Products (USOP), a publicly traded company, to acquire C-W-C.

Endeavoring to uphold the company's contract office furnishings focus and its dominance in the metro Atlanta market, C-W-C's existing management team repurchased the company back from USOP in October 2000. Presently guided by its five principals — Cindy Butler, Paul Conley, Scott Marshall, Dave Randolph, and Hal Brandon — C-W-C is now owned and operated by these five long-term employees and a group of employee shareholders. With their vested interest in C-W-C, these employees feel personally committed to upholding and enhancing the company's excellent reputation.

The result is that customers return to C-W-C time and time again due to the remarkable products and service they can expect. Regardless of the furnishings customers seek, they will likely find items to suit their needs in Atlanta's

largest showroom. Displaying a complete sampling of Herman Miller and Kimball Office products, as well as a vast array of additional quality lines, C-W-C's showroom has furnishing options appropriate to fit any customer's budget. The showroom also maintains a current library of product literature and fabric and finish samples enhancing what is displayed on the showroom floor.

Once a customer has selected quality furnishings from C-W-C, the top-notch service experience has just begun. In addition to delivering and installing furniture for customers, C-W-C's operations department goes the extra mile to ensure customer satisfaction. Installation and delivery can take place whenever the customer's schedule allows it — day, evening, or weekend. Each delivery and installation starts with a call from scheduling and ends with a call from quality assurance. C-W-C has a complete staff of field technicians including Mr. John Gouch who has been with the company for over 34 years in the branch of the department dedicated to handling repairs. C-W-C also employs full-time technicians equipped to handle general service and warranty challenges, providing reasonably priced repair service to extend the life of existing furniture. The operations department also offers affordable, secure customer storage at warehouse rates.

Along with its traditional furniture offerings, C-W-C offers customers several more in-depth services, including those of its talented, well-educated design team. C-W-C's designers remain up-to-date on the latest technological advancements in their field, working with clients to achieve an overall furniture plan and to meet project specifications. In working with the architectural and design community, C-W-C's design team strives to

enhance the relationship between the firm and the client by providing skilled knowledge of commercial furnishings and completing the detailed specifications.

C-W-C also proudly offers the expert services of its project management team, headed by Neil McTavish, who spent two decades as the corporate architect for a major Atlanta corporation. This staff has provided its broad spectrum of services for projects of all shapes and sizes — from hundreds of square feet to hundreds of thousands, from small schools to large universities and from small nonprofit organizations to large corporations. Available

...C-W-C's showroom has furnishing options appropriate to fit any customer's budget.

services include project scheduling and tracking, managing project flow, coordination of manufacturer deliveries, coordination with clients and designers, preparation of detailed punch lists, move management, and onsite facility services.

From its design and project management teams to its furniture showroom, C-W-C continues to operate under the same philosophy that it has had since 1929, providing the best products available coupled with unsurpassed service. From the first point of contact with a customer, C-W-C works to ensure that every phase of a project — however small or large — meets completion in its intended form and in a timely manner. Today's C-W-C upholds its longstanding tradition of not simply meeting, but exceeding its customers' expectations.

The Home Depot

The Home Depot is the world's largest home improvement retailer and the second-largest retailer in the United States, after Wal-Mart. The company was founded in 1978 by Bernie Marcus and Arthur Blank. Armed only with a concept, a small amount of money and a handful of like-minded friends, Bernie and Arthur opened the first three Home Depot stores in Atlanta in 1979. Those first three stores were built in space sublet from another retailer called Treasure Island.

Since that time, Home Depot has grown from those three stores, with 200 associates and $7 million in sales in its first year, to more than 1,500 stores, 300,000 associates and $58.2 billion in sales in 2002.

Home Depot's philosophy — building warehouse-style stores with a vast assortment of 40,000 different products at the lowest prices; backed with the best customer service in retail — continues to the present day. And, unlike other improvement retailers, Home Depot was designed to serve both do-it-yourselfers and professional contractors

Within its first five years, Home Depot had grown to dozens of stores, including new locations in Georgia, Florida, Louisiana, Texas and Alabama. Soon after, the company entered California, Arizona and the Northeastern United States. It opened its 1,000th store in June 2000, and now operates in all 50 states, Puerto Rico, eight Canadian provinces and Mexico, and maintains buying offices in China.

During the past 25 years, Home Depot also built a family of other home improvement concepts. The first of these was Expo Design Center, a 53-store chain that provides home decorating products and services to consumers and contractors. The

company also began two specialty concept chains, including Home Depot Landscape Supply for the landscape industry and Home Depot Supply for professional builders and contractors. Home Depot also acquired specialty outlets Georgia Lighting and National Blinds & Wallpaper; service order firms Maintenance Warehouse and Your "Other" Warehouse; and installation firms handling flooring, roofing, windows and siding.

The Home Depot group is credited with revolutionizing the home improvement retail industry. Its stores stock up to 40,000 different kinds of products in 12 retail categories including plumbing, electrical, lumber, millwork, paint, floor covering, building materials, lighting, appliances, garden and kitchen & bath. Its stores also provide inimitable services including free in-store clinics for honing home improvement skills, design and decorating consultation, truck and tool rental, home delivery, free potting and other services.

Home Depot stores rang up more than 1 billion customer transactions in a year for the first time in 2001, ranking it as the fastest-growing retailer in history — the first to reach $30 billion, then $40 billion and now $50 billion in sales — and the youngest retailer in the Fortune 50. More than 22 million customers visit Home Depot stores each week.

Home Depot is the largest retailer of flooring products in North America. In fact, the company sold enough carpeting in 2002 to pave a two lane road from Atlanta to Los Angeles to New York City and back to Atlanta again. Its stores sell enough paint in a year to cover the square footage of Manhattan Island with one good coat and still have enough left over to cover a good portion of Brooklyn. And if all the 2-inch disposable brushes Home Depot sells each year were lined up side-by-side, they would paint a stripe 1,622 miles wide — about the distance from New York City to Denver.

While Home Depot successfully presents customers with home improvement solutions, its good will does not stop there. In fact, Home Depot is the world's leading employer of Olympic and Paralympic athletes and hopefuls, where 20 Home Depot athlete-associates competed in the 2002 Olympic and Paralympic Winter Games in Salt Lake City and brought home eight medals. Furthermore, more than a half-million children have built their first toolbox at a Home Depot Kids Workshop.

Home Depot has received numerous accolades and much recognition for its contribution to the industry. Some of the awards it has earned include the title of High Growth Retailer in 1981 as named by Management Horizons; the

title of Retailer of the Year for the second time in 1988 as named by Building Supply Home Centers; the title of High Performance Retailer in 1988 for the seventh consecutive year as named by Management Horizons; the title of Growth Company of the Year in 1991 as named by National Association of Investors Corporation; and the President's National Community Service Award in 1995. Home Depot has also received the President's Sustainable Development Award — the nation's highest environmental honor — in 1996; the Vision for America Award in 1997 from Keep America Beautiful; and the Award for Excellence in Corporate Community Service in 1998 from Points of Light Foundation.

While Home Depot has helped many individuals from places everywhere with their home improvement needs, they can all thank the first three stores in Atlanta, Georgia, for getting the prized trend started. Now several projects, accomplishments and awards later, Home Depot relentlessly promises to help customers fix it, build it, grow it, decorate it and install it.

JW Marriott Buckhead Atlanta

It all started with a root beer stand in Washington, D.C. The year was 1927 and husband and wife, J. Willard and Alice S. Marriott, opened their nine-stool A&W Root Beer stand, naming it "The Hot Shoppe," and welcomed the public to enjoy refreshing treats and good company. After the couple introduced hot Mexican food items to the menu and invented curb service, Hot Shoppes, Inc. was officially incorporated. While the business's incorporation was promising, who would have thought that the simple stand would turn into one of the leading hospitality companies in the world?

For the next 58 years, until his death in August 1985, J. Willard Marriott rarely rested. He was constantly building his business by adding locations, perfecting procedures, or expanding into new enterprises. Setting a foundation as the hospitality leader his organization was to become, in 1939 Marriott landed his first food-service management contract with the U.S. Treasury. In addition, during World War II, Hot Shoppes fed thousands of workers who had relocated to the nation's capital to work in the defense industry. After the first Hot Shoppes cafeteria was established at McLean Gardens in Washington, D.C. in 1945, it managed to land its first government feeding contract the same year. A mere decade later, new enterprises progressed — Marriott Food Service secured its first institutional and school feeding contracts at Children's Hospital and American University, and Marriott's Highway Division opened several Hot Shoppes on the New Jersey Turnpike.

Gradually evolving from Hot Shoppes, Inc. to Marriott Corporation, the company opened its first hotel, a 365-room Twin Bridges Motor Hotel in Arlington, Virginia, in 1957. Then in 1964 J.W. Marriott, Jr. was named president of the organization. Throughout his presidency, J.W. Marriott, Jr. has taken Marriott from a family restaurant business to a $19-billion global lodging company with 2,700 properties in 70 countries. Mr. Marriott envisions Marriott as the world's leading provider of hospitality services; he believes in taking care of guests, extensive operational knowledge, the development of a highly skilled and diverse work force, and offering the best portfolio of lodging brands in the industry. Under his leadership, Marriott continues to enjoy strong customer, owner and franchise preference, steady growth and profitability.

A division of what is now Marriott International, today's Marriott® Hotels & Resorts bestows a new dimension of luxury, featuring exquisite architectural detail, the finest dining, and gracious sophistication for guests. With a sincere desire to make stays as comfortable and productive as they are luxurious, the company works 24 hours a day, every day, to serve guests through its business center, concierge, valet, and room service associates — however and whenever they wish.

JW Marriott Hotels & Resorts, named for J.W. Marriott, Jr., includes 31 luxury properties located in great gateway city centers and upscale resort locations throughout the world. In the Asia-Pacific, the company has hotels and resorts in:

- Bangkok, Thailand;
- Hong Kong, China;
- Jakarta, Indonesia;
- Kuala Lumpur, Malaysia;
- Mumbai, India;
- Phuket, Thailand;
- Seoul, South Korea;
- Shanghai, China;
- and Surabaya, Indonesia.

In the Middle East and South America there are establishments in:

- Cairo, Egypt;
- Dubai, United Arab Emirates;
- Kuwait, Kuwait;
- Caracas, Venezuela;
- Lima, Peru;
- Quito, Ecuador;
- and Rio de Janeiro, Brazil.

Throughout North America, travelers can find JW Marriott presence in Atlanta, Georgia; Cancun, Mexico; Houston, Texas; Ko Olina, Hawaii; Las Vegas, Nevada; Mexico City, Mexico; Miami, Florida; and New Orleans, Louisiana. Operations also exist in New York, New York; Orlando, Florida; Palm Desert, California; Phoenix, Arizona; Santa Monica, California; and Washington, D.C.

JW Marriott Hotels & Resorts, named for J.W. Marriott, Jr., includes 31 luxury properties located in great gateway city centers and upscale resort locations throughout the world.

While all have welcoming and distinctive environments, the JW Marriott Buckhead Atlanta offers comfortable luxury in Atlanta's most cosmopolitan business, shopping, dining and entertainment community known as "Buckhead." Directly connected to the premier shopping of Lenox Square Mall and one block from exquisite shops of Phipps Plaza, the establishment was designed to surpass the demands of today's sophisticated traveler. Thus, the JW Marriott Buckhead Atlanta offers 371 elegantly appointed room accommodations including four luxurious suites, each enhanced with award-winning service and meticulous attention to detail. Conveniently located in the heart of Buckhead, it is just a short MARTA train ride to Midtown, Downtown, and Atlanta's Hartsfield Airport. For both business and leisure travelers, the JW Marriott Hotel Buckhead Atlanta fulfills the needs of each and every one of its guests.

Despite its large-scale size, Marriott Hotels & Resorts has managed to retain the core values established by the Marriott family over 75 years ago. With the enduring belief that its associates are its greatest assets, the "Marriott Way" is built on the "Spirit to Serve" customers and its enveloping communities.

As part of this spirit, Marriott Hotels & Resorts maintains an environment that supports associate growth and personal development, a reputation for employing caring and dependable associates who are ethical and trustworthy, and an inviting workplace that facilitates rewarding relationships. The company also implements a performance-recognition system that commemorates both hourly and management associates and keeps a focus on growth-managed and franchised properties, owners and investors.

Possessing pride in the Marriott name, its accomplishments, and its record of success, Marriott Hotels & Resorts considers the customer always right, executes a hands-on management style, pays great attention to detail, and knows that customers count on its unique mixture of quality, consistency, personalized service and recognition. In addition, this spirit of conducting business the "Marriott Way" is embodied in the company's associate and corporate support of local, national and international initiatives and programs.

From the beginning, Marriott's common culture has been based on taking care of its employees so that they take care of customers. Because this culture has positively influenced the way the multinational corporation treats its

...the "Marriott Way" is built on the "Spirit to Serve" customers and its enveloping communities.

associates, customers and the communities that impact all of its successes, it has never failed to promote the words of J.W. Marriott, Jr. when he said, "culture is the life-thread and glue that links our past, present and future." It is through such a perspective and resulting prosperity that Marriott International, Marriott Hotels & Resorts, and JW Marriott Buckhead Atlanta have qualified the company as one of the greatest hospitality outfits in the world.

Renaissance Concourse

Opportunely located next to the Hartsfield-Jackson Atlanta International Airport, the Renaissance Concourse Hotel offers guests a welcoming and comfortable environment to accommodate their varying traveling needs. Sitting spectacularly on the former site of the airport's original terminal building, the hotel can be found at Hartsfield Centre complex, only moments away from Georgia International Convention Center, Downtown Atlanta and Georgia World Congress Center. A $50 million structure with an innovative acoustical design that minimizes airport noise, the newly renovated 11-story, 387-room hotel offers an uncompromising level of excellent personal service and first-class amenities.

Among a number of conveniences, the hotel has in-room dining, complimentary airport shuttle service, gift shop, concierge, and on-site laundry and valet service. In addition, spacious guest rooms and suites; adorned meeting and conference facilities; and a trained staff of dedicated professionals conjointly create an overall obliging atmosphere for all guests to enjoy.

Guests will find the Renaissance Concourse adorned with exclusive artwork reminiscent of the "old south" and a grand staircase that will make them feel like they stepped onto the set of *Gone with the Wind*. As guests walk through the atrium level of the hotel, they can admire the

> **For luxurious exclusivity, guests of the Renaissance Concourse can also reserve a room on the private Renaissance Club Level.**

classic scenery: plantation gardens and gazebos abounded with beautiful live trees, an open-air backdrop and an unparalleled view of the neighboring airport's runways.

Renaissance Concourse Hotel's newly renovated guest rooms come beautifully decorated and equipped with comfortable seating areas and roomy bathrooms. Rooms also offer visitors an over-sized desk; a sofa or lounge chair; direct-dial telephones with data ports; and a remote-controlled color television featuring complimentary high-speed Internet access, cable stations and box-office release movies available on a pay-per-view basis. Additional services include complimentary in-room coffee and weekday newspaper delivery. If desired, guests can also stay in one of the hotel's four luxury suites, which feature parlors, two bathrooms and two balconies. Guests also have the option of staying in one of the 150 balcony rooms that directly overlook the airport or one of the 350 non-smoking rooms.

For luxurious exclusivity, guests of the Renaissance Concourse can also reserve a room on the private Renaissance Club Level. Accessed by private key entry only, rooms offer a special concierge service and admission to the private Club Lounge, which serves complimentary deluxe continental breakfast and evening hors d'oeuvres Monday through Friday. Within each room, guests also receive complimentary water and other amenities such as evening turndown service and spacious bathrooms with access to a telephone, a television, a weight scale and bathrobes. Complete with rich cherry wood doors and prominent wall-coverings, the private Renaissance Club Level imparts sophistication and satisfaction to the most discerning hotel guests.

Renaissance Concourse provides three levels and 34,000 square feet of 28 meeting rooms, including the superlative 11,000-square-foot Concourse Ballroom, which is the largest airport hotel ballroom in the country; five distinguished permanent boardrooms, two spacious pre-function areas; and an elegant private dining room. For attendee convenience, select meeting spaces offer telephones and conversation areas with windows that offer dazzling views of the grand staircase and atrium. Each meeting room also includes individual lighting controls; hidden electrical and sound systems to minimize cord clutter; capabilities to accommodate groups with heavy electrical telephone and computer requirements; high-speed internet access; conference call capabilities; a fully equipped Business Center for complete secretarial services; and an in-house Audio-Visual Department. Spanning all conference and banquet facilities is a renowned staff of experienced event managers, and convention service and catering professionals that will oversee every detail for any business-related or other special event held at the Renaissance.

For dining and entertainment, Renaissance boasts an intimate lounge — the Concorde Bar —where cocktails are served while guests can observe powerful runway takeoffs,

simply chat with one another, or watch an evening sporting event. For a heightened dining experience, guests and other patrons can also relish in refined-yet-casual, all-day, contemporary American cuisine with a Mediterranean flair at the Concorde Grill. With fine food and beverages such as fresh-squeezed juices, gourmet salads and nightly specials; 40 different wines and dozens of imported and domestic beers; attentive service; a private, antique furnished dining room — the Candler Room; and wondrous views, the restaurant is readily prepared to pamper guests and serve all types of taste buds.

Recreationally, guests can take advantage of the hotel's 3,000 square feet of free weights and advanced, computerized fitness equipment; its designated men's and women's locker, sauna and steam rooms; and its indoor — with a skylight that permits natural sunlight and starlight to enter — and outdoor swimming pools to cover the different seasons throughout the year. By combining all of the offered exercise and relaxation options, guests can exit the facilities with a satisfied feeling of thorough rejuvenation.

With a convenient location, breathtaking views, gorgeous rooms and superior accommodations, Renaissance Concourse Hotel tends to guests with the hospitality and care that Southerners are known for. Through its plethora of complimentary services, wide-range of rooming and dining options, and highly competent and courteous staff, the hotel ensures a memorable stay to all those who visit Atlanta.

Rich's-Macy's

THEN AND NOW

The story of Rich's began in Atlanta with a young immigrant whose vigor and optimism matched the city's own.

In 1867, 20-year-old Morris Rich saw an opportunity to help the devastated city rise from the ashes of the Civil War. He borrowed $500 from his brother William and opened a small retail dry goods store with five employees on Whitehall Street. The first year's sales volume was

$5,000 and delivery was by a mule and wagon. Today Rich's-Macy's, a division of Federated Department Stores, Inc., is part of a national network of 459 department stores in 34 states, Guam and Puerto Rico under the names of Macy's, Bloomingdale's, Bon-Macy's, Burdines-Macy's, Goldsmith's-Macy's, Lazarus-Macy's and Rich's-Macy's with retail sales topping $15.2 billion.

THROUGH THE YEARS

In 1924 the store moved to Broad Street and in 1948 the home store was added, connected to the main store by a crystal bridge. That same year, the first great tree was lit.

In 1959 Rich's opened its Lenox Square store at the first major suburban mall built in Atlanta, keeping in line with the city's suburban growth. As the city has grown so has Rich's-Macy's, now with 17 stores in the metro area. In 2000 a multimillion-dollar renovation made Rich's-Macy's at Lenox Square the division's flagship store — demonstrating its ability to meet the ever-changing needs and desires of its diverse customer base.

A new era began when Federated Department Stores acquired Rich's in 1976. Federated Department Stores, Inc. is the nation's largest operator of department stores with 459 department stores located in 34 states. In 1995 Federated selected Rich's for the corporate headquarters of its Rich's/Lazarus/Goldsmith division. From the Atlanta headquarters, the RLG-M division operates more than 77 stores in nine states including 29 Rich's-Macy's stores in metro Atlanta, Augusta, Savannah, Athens, Columbus and Macon, Georgia; Birmingham, Alabama; and Columbia and Greenville, South Carolina. The combined Rich's-Macy's in metro Atlanta employs 5,500 people.

THE MERGING OF TWO RETAIL ICONS

In 2003 Federated Department Stores initiated a strategic integration of its stores in metro Atlanta by extending the powerful Macy's brand to the established hometown favorite Rich's. Rich's-Macy's is now part of Federated Department Stores, Inc. initiative to reinvent the department store. The reinvent strategies have been designed to enhance the shopping experience by offering a unique and differentiated merchandise mix along with friendly, knowledgeable customer service. Some highlights include comfortable lounge areas, enhanced fitting rooms, innovative merchandising with an emphasis on exclusive private labels like INC, Alfani, Charter Club and Style & Co. Rich's-Macy's has also added supervised children's play areas in several locations. The main goal is to offer customers a convenient and easy store to shop.

TIME TO CELEBRATE

Over the years Rich's made Atlanta history by turning events into traditions. Generations of Atlanta children celebrated the holidays with the Lighting of the Rich's

Great Tree and a ride on Rich's Pink Pig, a monorail with porcine appeal that circled the rooftop of Rich's downtown store. Today these traditions continue. The Lighting of the Rich's-Macy's Great Tree brings thousands of families together as they celebrate Thanksgiving. In 2003 Rich's-Macy's reintroduced Priscilla the Pink Pig, enabling parents and grandparents to carry on family traditions by taking their children on the ride they remembered fondly.

A GREAT PLACE TO SHOP, A WONDERFUL NEIGHBOR TO HAVE

From the very beginning, Morris Rich believed that his department store was more than a collection of merchandise. Rich's philosophy was to put the people — both customers and employees — first. This became apparent in 1917 when a terrible fire raced through 73 blocks of Atlanta, wiping out 1,553 homes. Rich's employees helped to fight the fire and the store offered clothing and household goods to the families who'd lost everything in the blaze. This spirit of generosity continued through the depression and is very much a part of Rich's-Macy's legacy today.

A community leader in the United Way and one of the largest business contributors to the Atlanta Community Food Bank, Rich's-Macy's has also raised millions of dollars

for nonprofit organizations through iconic events like the Lighting of the Rich's Great Tree and Priscilla the Pink Pig, fashion shows, special events and promotions with the core emphasis on children and education, women's health issues, AIDS/HIV prevention and support and the arts.

In 1998 Rich's and Piedmont Hospital joined together to open a permanent mammography center at Rich's Perimeter Mall location. In partnership with the American Heart Association and its Go Red for Women campaign, Rich's-Macy's is raising awareness and funds for the growing concern of women and heart disease.

PARTNERS IN TIME CELEBRATES 15 YEARS OF SHARING AND CARING

Rich's-Macy's Partners in Time, an employee volunteer force started in 1989, allows employees and their families and friends to share their time and talents in community-wide volunteer projects. Rich's-Macy's associates volunteer 36,000 hours annually in company-sponsored projects. The White House recognized Partners in Time with its Volunteer Action Award in 1991 and Rich's received the IMPACT Award from the Points of Light Foundation and Colin Powel in 1998. Additionally, in 2004 the program broke the 1 million volunteer-hour mark for all of Federated Department Stores.

Rich's-Macy's is at the heart of Atlanta, a trusted resource that generations of customers have relied on. It's not hard to find shoppers with their own family stories of promises kept, services rendered and satisfactions enjoyed from Rich's-Macy's over the years. Whether native or newcomer, Rich's-Macy's is the store that knows how to celebrate Southern style.

Waffle House

More than 200 bright yellow Waffle House® signs dot the metropolitan Atlanta skyline welcoming travelers and regular diners alike. Waffle House restaurants' No.1 priority is to take care of the customer by serving Good Food Fast®. The extensive menu of quality food items includes waffles, T-bone steaks, omelets, USDA Choice hamburgers, hashbrowns, and grits. Each top-quality meal is concocted from the finest, freshest ingredients, cooked to order and served on real china with fast-food speed by a friendly, welcoming staff.

The Waffle House story started 50 years ago when two neighbors decided to create a unique, people-oriented restaurant with great food at a terrific value. Joe Rogers, Sr. and Tom Forkner opened the first Waffle House restaurant on Labor Day in 1955 in Avondale Estates, Georgia. With its enthusiastic group of associates and terrific food, the restaurant quickly picked up a loyal, local clientele. The company began to expand throughout Georgia and into neighboring states. Today there are more than 1,400 Waffle House restaurants in 25 states, with territories extending as far north as Pennsylvania and as far west as Arizona.

Waffle House restaurants' yellow signs have become an American icon.

Waffle House restaurants' yellow signs have become an American icon. Known as America's Place to Eat®, Waffle House is the world's leading server of waffles, raisin toast, T-bone steaks, USDA Choice hamburgers, hashbrowns, and grits, just to name a few. The restaurants serve only top brands such as Coca-Cola soft drinks, Jimmy Dean sausages, the complete line of sauces from Heinz, Wishbone salad dressings and pastries straight from the

Tom Forkner and Joe Rogers, Sr., founders of Waffle House, Inc., visit an Atlanta-area restaurant.

kitchens of Sara Lee. Among its other remarkable statistics Waffle House restaurants have served more than 440 million waffles since 1955 and serve over 95 million cups of coffee each year. Although breakfast is served at any hour of the day, diners need not fear monotony on the menu. When challenged to find as many ways as possible to prepare USDA Choice hamburgers, Waffle House restaurants responded with more than 70 million mouth-watering concoctions.

What else makes the Waffle House experience distinctive? For starters Waffle House aficionados need not check the hours on their favorite eating establishment. Every Waffle House restaurant is open 24 hours a day, seven days a week, 365 days a year, making it a great option for late night dining or an early morning cup of coffee. In addition, the kitchens are located in full view of the restaurant, allowing customers to see their orders being prepared. When walking into a Waffle House, no matter what time of day, customers are not only greeted by an amiable staff and a menu filled with delicious food, but also with songs from the now famous Waffle House jukebox. Memorable songs include "Waffle Doo Wop" and "Waffle House Family."

Though alike in so many ways, each individual Waffle House restaurant succeeds due to a motivated group of people — the associates — working together as a team. The son of co-founder Joe Rogers, Sr. — Joe Rogers, Jr. — now runs Waffle House, Inc. He continues the tradition started by his father and Tom Forkner that has made Waffle House not only America's Place to Eat®, but also America's Place to Work®. Having started working for Waffle House bussing tables as a young boy, Joe Rogers, Jr. became president of the company in 1973 at the age of 26. To this day he spends most of his time out in the field at different Waffle Houses, continuing the company's focus on people.

Each company restaurant is employee-owned and owner-managed, with both hourly and management employees given the opportunity to purchase stock in the company. In addition Waffle House offers health benefits, incentive-based compensation, and bonuses to both management and hourly employees. With so much attention on its associates, it is no wonder that making Waffle House a long-term career choice has been easy for a large number of employees. The employees, in turn, care deeply about making each individual meal served part of the greater Waffle House success story.

Headquartered in Norcross, Georgia, Waffle House invites customers from all walks of life to partake in the delicious dining experience available at each and every one of its restaurants. From celebrities such as Faith Hill, Billy Bob Thornton, Beyonce Knowles, former President George Bush, Amy Grant and Emmitt Smith — all who have been seen eating at Waffle House — to construction workers, nurses, families and CEOs, Waffle House has come to be enjoyed over and over again by its customers. The food, the music and the experience all combine together to create the Unique American Phenomenon™ that is Waffle House.

AMERICASMART®▪ATLANTA

AMERICASMART▪ATLANTA is the world's largest and most comprehensive wholesale marketplace. In essence, AMERICASMART is a shopping mall for retailers.

The who's who of retailing worldwide comes to AMERICASMART▪ATLANTA to shop its 6.2 million square feet of showrooms and temporary booths, housing 4.2 million square feet of new and innovative merchandise. The product selection — all under one roof and all at one time — is unequaled, and admission to AMERICASMART▪ATLANTA is available only to qualified buyers. Everything from the exotic and one-of-a-kind, to lifestyle product essentials is among the merchandise, and buyers come from all 50 U.S. states and 80 countries to buy the gift, home furnishings and decor, area rug and apparel industries' hottest products.

AMERICASMART▪ATLANTA is owned by AMC, Inc., a dominant player in the worldwide multibillion-dollar wholesale trade and retail industry. The world's largest trade mart and trade show company, AMC's principal business unit and flagship is AMERICASMART▪ATLANTA. Led by founder and Chairman John C. Portman, Jr., AMERICASMART traces its origins to 1957. It is today the nation's number-one and growing gift, home furnishings and area rug marketplace and the preferred market for a burgeoning number of apparel retailers.

In the heart of downtown Atlanta, AMERICASMART▪ATLANTA comprises three buildings: AMERICASMART ❶ (formerly known as the Merchandise Mart), AMERICASMART ❷ (formerly known as the Gift Mart) and AMERICASMART ❸ (formerly known as the Apparel Mart). It hosts 23 markets annually and six Market Wednesdays. The Markets include both permanent and temporary product components. Between Market hours are held Monday through Friday the remainder of the year.

Among the specialty product centers found at AMERICASMART▪ATLANTA are gift, home accents and furnishings, home accents and fine linens, holiday, floral and home décor, The Gardens®, area rug, apparel, fashion accessories and fine jewelry, gourmet, as well as resort and souvenir gift. Product also is available at Market in temporary booths presented in 17 distinctive merchandise categories.

Through the years, retailers attending its markets have cited AMERICASMART▪ATLANTA as the marketplace most important to their businesses as compared to all other markets in independent research. But AMERICASMART is just as essential to Atlanta's convention business and has become both a downtown anchor and a landmark.

From its early days and through the millennium and beyond, AMERICASMART▪ATLANTA is a mainstay on the wholesale front. As an international cornerstone in a multibillion-dollar industry, AMERICASMART is a unique addition to this international city. As the brainchild of a local businessman, architect, developer and visionary, it is representative of the dreams and accomplishments of the city's own people and their impact on the world.

(Left) AMERICASMART hosts 23 wholesale markets and six Market Wednesdays that annually attract more than 548,000 attendees from every U.S. state and 80 countries.

(Right) Led by founder and Chairman John C. Portman, Jr., AMERICASMART▪ATLANTA is the nation's leading wholesale market center.

Portman Holdings, L.P.

Portman Holdings, L.P., the international real estate development arm of the Portman Companies, was established to capitalize on more than 40 years of experience in real estate development, management and finance. Serving clients around the world from its headquarters in Atlanta, the Portman organization brings creativity and vision to the design and development of successful real estate. Acting solely, and in conjunction

Sun Trust Plaza — Atlanta, Georgia
Photo by Timothy Hursley

> **By utilizing a unique combination of creativity, tenacity and experience, Portman Holdings helps its clients excel in the competitive real estate market.**

with investors, Portman Holdings has developed 16,000 hotel rooms, 16 office buildings, over 1 million square feet of retail space and more than 10 million square feet of marts/exhibition space worldwide.

Portman Holdings offers a single source for all phases of the real estate development process. From conception through ongoing management of the project, Portman Holdings provides systematic, sequential development services, and long-term investment opportunities for international and domestic business owners. By employing an effective and profitable combination of architecture and development, Portman Holdings has initiated significant urban redevelopments, which have served as catalysts for renewal in major international cities. Utilizing a unique combination of creativity, tenacity and experience, Portman Holdings helps its clients excel in the competitive real estate market.

Interior view of the newly completed Westin Hotel in Warsaw, Poland
Photo by Jaime Ardilles-Arce

"In a region as fast-growing and diverse at ours, the biggest challenge to MARTA is meeting the multiplying transportation needs of the area's residents. But MARTA is about more than buses and trains; it's also about clearing the air, improving traffic congestion and improving the quality of life for everyone."

Nathaniel P. Ford Sr., GM/CEO
MARTA

"Southern Company and its subsidiary companies have been among Atlanta's leading corporate citizens for more than a century. We have taken great pride in being active participants in Atlanta's growth and development as a world-class city. We look forward to continuing our commitment to the enhancement of Atlanta and its people."

David Ratcliffe, Chairman, President, CEO
Southern Company

NETWORKS & TRANSPORTATION

A hub of transportation and a premier location for cutting-edge media and utilities, Atlanta is home to a wealth of organizations that keep information, people, products and power moving throughout the region and the world.

MARTA

Reliable and efficient, MARTA (Metropolitan Atlanta Rapid Transit Authority) is the ninth-largest transit system in the United States and North America. Providing all-access public transportation — via bus, rail, and paratransit (designed for eligible individuals whose disabilities prevent them from using fixed-route services) — the organization operates through 4,300 employees and transports an average of a half-million passengers daily. To put its overall number of passengers into perspective, since 1979, MARTA has transported approximately 3.5 billion people, which is 10 times the entire population of the United States.

Covering a multitude of routes, MARTA operates 691 buses that travel 1,128 miles per day and 31 million miles per year, 110 paratransit vans that average 275,000 hours per year, and 338 rail cars that pass through 38 stations on 47.6 miles of rail. Serving 1,854,338 riders throughout the city of Atlanta and Fulton and DeKalb counties, in fiscal year 2003 alone, MARTA's trains and buses provided over 65.5 million passenger trips.

MARTA was the first agency to engage in a transit-oriented development project — MARTA partnered with BellSouth Corporation to participate in the premier Transit Oriented Development (TOD), which linked transit with communities to provide alternatives to congested highways — the result: Lindbergh City Center, a blend of commercial, residential, and retail developments that is the largest multi-use development of its kind in the United States. MARTA is also the U.S. transit agency with the third-largest compressed natural gas-propelled bus fleet and the first agency to provide direct access to a major airline, Delta,

in one of its 38 rail stations. As is evident, MARTA has encountered many milestones. Such advancement does not come easily, though; it takes a wealth of history and an ambitious nature to get there. These are two characteristics that MARTA has possessed since its original conception in 1952.

In 1952, Atlanta's Regional Planning guide recognized the effect that mass transit could have on regional growth. In support of such a concept, the Metropolitan Planning Commission (MPC) inaugurated a series of transportation policy studies. Atlanta Transit System published "Rapid Atlanta," which was the first proposal for a specific rapid transit system; and ARMPC published "What You Should Know about Rapid Transit" and "Atlanta Regional Comprehensive Plan: Rapid Transit" in 1961. In response to the movement and in support of the conducted studies, a Georgia House Resolution formed the Metropolitan Atlanta Transit Study Commission (MATSC) to conduct its own study program to report the need, advisability, and economic feasibility of implementing a rapid mass transportation system. It was essentially because of MATSC's published "A Plan and Program of Rapid Transit for the Atlanta Metropolitan Region," which recommended a 66-mile, five-county rail system with feeder bus operation and park-and-ride facilities, and the formation of "The Rapid Transit Committee of 100" created to inform metropolitan citizens of the importance of rapid transit, that the Georgia State Legislature formed the Georgia State Study Commission on Rapid Transit to examine the notion for the State's point of view.

When the Metropolitan Atlanta Rapid Transit Authority Act became a law in 1965, having passed the Georgia General Assembly 205 to 12, the rapid transit concept was on the verge of realization. Once the local referendum ratifying participation in the Transit Authority succeeded in four counties and the City of Atlanta, MARTA was created by the Act in March of 1965 and

established as an agency. In 1968 the Atlanta Area Transportation Study Policy Committee held its first meeting to finish the development of a comprehensive, balanced and long-range regional transportation plan. By March of that year preliminary engineering on a basic 21-mile system had been completed, and further funding resulted in the "Town Flyer" project, which allowed passengers to park outside the congested downtown area and ride designated buses into the central business district.

In August 1971 MARTA assumed control of the Model Cities Shuttle Bus Service and a year later it not only received a grant from DOT/UMTA to fund two-thirds of its system's final design and environmental analysis studies, but it also purchased the Atlanta Transit System for $12,958,074. Such progress, along with its acquisition of 125 new, air-conditioned buses, helped MARTA begin execution on five of seven planned new radial routes that included service to Alpharetta, Palmetto, and Lithonia. By March 1973 MARTA had carried a total of 65,543,400 passengers — a 21 percent increase and 11.5 million more than the previous year. Then in June, Secretary of Transportation Claude S. Brinegar approved a $69.5 million grant to MARTA to help finance the first phase of construction and design on its 50-mile rapid rail and 14-mile busway system. In 1974 the first rapid rail system architectural and engineering design consultant teams were selected, resulting in an aerial structure selected for use on more than 10.1 miles of the 62.9-mile rapid rail system.

A celebrated occasion in MARTA's history was in August 1971 when it started construction on its airport rapid rail station. In association with Hartsfield Atlanta International Airport — the only airport in North America to offer convenient train-to-plane service — MARTA inaugurated feeder service by diverting its bus line to feed into the airport-located station. In fact, at this time, the transportation organization diverted almost all of its bus lines to feed into various stations.

Over many years of operation MARTA has been awarded a plethora of awards in recognition of its outstanding service in a variety of categories. It won Fleet Owner Magazine's "Maintenance Award" for the best-maintained fleet in the United States; the 1979 National Society of Professional Engineers' "Engineering Achievement Award" for MARTA's design and construction of the rapid rail system; and the 1980 award for design from the South Atlantic Regional Council of the American Institute of Architects. Of extremely noteworthy importance, MARTA was also declared "the safest system in the United States among cities with a population of one million and over" by American Public Transit Association (APTA) in 1981. In addition, that same year, Governor George Busbee signed a proclamation commending MARTA for "...the improvements it had brought to the lives of its users, and for the renowned dependability of its service."

MARTA released a new publication, MARTA 2000. This publication intended to summarize what had been accomplished by the organization and note what still needed to be done.

One of many ways in which MARTA has successfully progressed was when it agreed to join Amtrak, Greyhound, and a commuter rail system in one central station in May 1991. This breakthrough came to fruition when UMTA underwrote a study for a major passenger terminal in downtown Atlanta. In addition in March 1996, MARTA ranked as the busiest transit system in North America as it completed over 20 major projects in time for the Olympic Games. Proudly participating as an Atlanta agent, some regular bus routes operated 24 hours a day during the event for the first time in history. Once the 1996 Centennial Olympic Games officially began, MARTA was responsible for transporting all spectators to Olympic venues. Having completed all projects and improvements on time and before the Opening Ceremony, MARTA carried 17.8 million passengers in 17 days — an undertaking that typically took six weeks to attain. The end result: local, national and international accolades for the organization's overall success.

Then Atlanta encountered the Paralympic Games, which took place from August 15-25, 1996. As the "Official Ride to the Paralympic Games," MARTA pledged to customers that it would offer the greatest level of service and gave riders the opportunity to complete postcards that noted where improvements could be made. To complement this rider feedback, MARTA opened a customer hotline to gather information that would be used to solve both immediate and long-range issues.

MARTA is among only 10 transit agencies in the United States and Canada to have received the "APTA Job Access" award, which it did in May 2003. Its many awards, combined with the recognition it received when 11 MARTA women were honored at the 2003 YWCA Women of Achievement Luncheon and Benefit, complement the immense community service that it's engaged in quite well.

For over 25 years MARTA has been serving the community not only through transportation and environmental challenges, but also through charitable efforts. In fact, its Charity Club has raised an estimated $600,000 annually from

MARTA was also given the first ETZIE award by the Association of Retired Employees of America "for publicly acknowledging the value of the service rendered by its (MARTA's) retirees," and in June 1983 the organization won the New York Association of Consulting Engineers' "Certificate of Engineering Excellence." Then APTA gave MARTA its "Management Innovation Award" in November 1983.

MARTA has enforced and represented safety since its very beginning. Having increased its safety capabilities numerous times, it did so again in all of its rail stations in January 1986. As a result, MARTA won APTA's 1988 award for being the safest bus system in America. What's more, by 1995 the transportation organization had received APTA's "Safety Award" 17 out of 18 times.

In April 1990 MARTA's Long Range Planning Committee declared its support for a proposed state policy on public transit, including financial assistance for public transit. A nice birthday present, considering that MARTA was celebrating its 25th anniversary. To commemorate the milestone,

employee donations and volunteer efforts, making the dedicated group of MARTA employees one of Atlanta's major contributors for both Atlanta and surrounding communities. MARTA's Charity Club is responsible for linking employees to nonprofit organizations and resources that provide goods and services to the socio-economically disadvantaged. The Charity Club prides itself in providing the metropolitan Atlanta community with over 6,000 hours of community service through food and shelter initiatives.

So whether riders are residents or visitors looking to enjoy a Braves, Falcons, Thrashers, or Hawks game; get a ride home after a night on the town; spend a day at Atlanta's premier Six Flags amusement park; or catch a plane, MARTA is a perfect option. With historical and award-winning testaments to its reliability and contribution, MARTA is a welcoming ride on a bus, train, or for paratransit that saves cents, and makes sense as well.

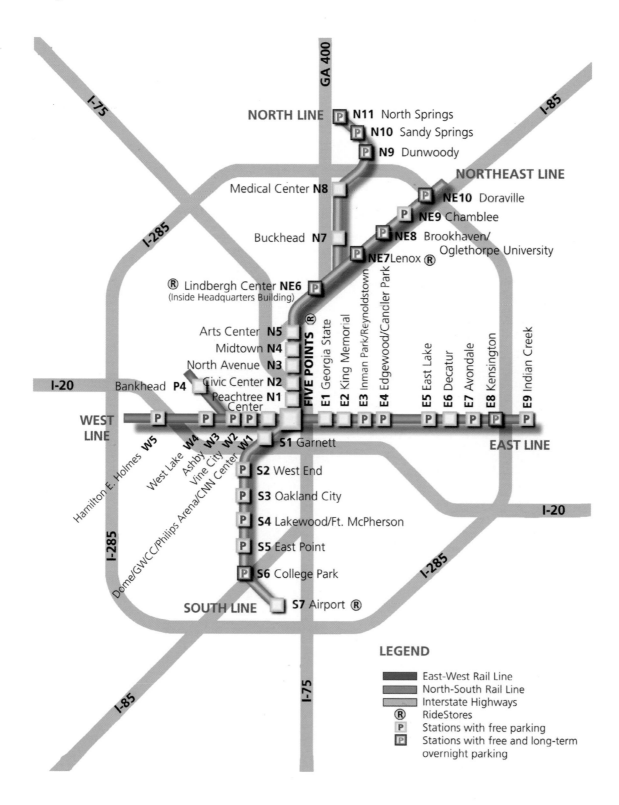

LEGEND

- East-West Rail Line
- North-South Rail Line
- Interstate Highways
- ® RideStores
- P Stations with free parking
- P Stations with free and long-term overnight parking

Southern Company

Southern Company is the premier energy company in the Southeast, serving more than 4 million customers in a region that stretches from the mountains of north Georgia through Alabama and northwest Florida to Mississippi's Gulf Coast.

As the parent firm of Georgia Power, Alabama Power, Gulf Power, Mississippi Power and Savannah Electric, Southern Company supplies energy to more than 12 million people in this fast-growing region. Its customers range from individuals in homes and apartments, to municipalities and vast manufacturing operations. With nearly 39,000 megawatts of generating capacity and more than 28,000 miles of high-voltage transmission lines, Southern Company is one of the nation's largest electricity producers.

David Ratcliffe is chairman, president and CEO of Southern Company, whose corporate headquarters is located in the heart of downtown Atlanta. The company generates more than 180 billion kilowatt-hours of electricity annually.

Other Southern Company subsidiaries include: Southern Power, a growing competitive generation company; Southern Nuclear, a nuclear plant operations subsidiary; Southern Company GAS, a competitive retail natural gas business; Southern Company Energy Solutions, an energy services business; Southern LINC, a wireless communications service; and Southern Telecom, a fiber optics business connecting Atlanta with smaller cities throughout the Southeast.

Southern Company is certainly big — it has annual operating revenues of more than $11 billion — but what's more important is the company's reputation for doing what it says it will do, for keeping its promises.

For the 10-year period ending in 2003, Southern Company's total shareholder return, which includes stock price appreciation and dividend reinvestment, averaged more than 14 percent a year. By comparison, the Standard & Poor's Electric Utilities Index had an average return of 6 percent a year. It's no wonder more than 500,000 shareholders own Southern Company stock (NYSE: SO), making it one of the most widely held stocks in America.

Such strong financial performance is one reason Southern Company has been named America's most admired electric and gas utility by *Fortune* magazine for three years in a row. The other reasons are embedded within the company's culture. Since its early days in the first half of the 20th century, Southern Company has always had a reputation for trying to do what is right within the communities it serves.

A CHANGING INDUSTRY

The electric utility landscape has changed dramatically in the past decade. The industry has seen California's catastrophic experiment with retail deregulation and the fall of Enron and other high-profile companies, as well as a crisis in credibility throughout corporate America.

What happened in California and what happened to Enron has changed the business parameters for all energy companies. Retail electricity deregulation has moved to the back burner and in some states has been reversed, energy trading has fallen off sharply and the industry has seen a decline in the merchant power plant business.

At about the same time that California's experiment with deregulation was changing the external environment for many utilities, Southern Company also was changing itself internally. Over a period of years in the 1990s, the company built one of the world's largest independent power producers in its Southern Energy subsidiary. It also continued to operate its five traditional utilities in the Southeast and, as a result, had two very different types of business in one company and in one stock.

Investors seeking a traditional utility stock were not interested in the growth potential coupled with higher risk of Southern Energy. They were more interested in the steady growth and performance of a regulated utility that pays a safe and consistent dividend — as Southern Company has every quarter for 56 years. Meanwhile, investors seeking growth were more interested in pure-play growth companies, with stock price appreciation versus current dividends. As a result, there was a large gap between the market value of the company and the value of the sum of its parts.

That's why Southern Company decided to spin off Mirant (the new name given to Southern Energy) to shareholders in the spring of 2001. Both companies performed well following the spin, until the fallout from Enron created problems for all companies heavily involved in energy trading and merchant power plants. The negative effect on Mirant and other companies in this sector has been significant.

A ROCK-SOLID STRATEGY

Since the spin-off, Southern Company has focused its business strategy on the Southeast and on two main businesses — regulated retail utilities and competitive generation. What distinguishes Southern Company from some of its peers is that it is willing to stick to the basics: the generation and delivery of electricity.

"We have a great strategy. It's working very well," says David Ratcliffe, Southern Company's new chairman, president and CEO. Ratcliffe served as president and CEO of the company's Georgia Power subsidiary before becoming Southern Company's CEO in July 2004 when Allen Franklin retired.

Southern Company's regulated retail utilities, which contribute more than 85 percent of its earnings, add thousands of new customers each year and are the company's foundation. And, thanks to Southern Company's reputation for first-class customer service, its competitive

With nearly 39,000 megawatts of generating capacity and more than 28,000 miles of high-voltage transmission lines, Southern Company is one of the largest electricity producers in the nation. The company's strong brand name has been associated with first-class customer service for many decades. That commitment has enabled the company to receive the highest rating of any utility company in the American Customer Satisfaction Index.

generation business — the company's primary growth vehicle — is exceeding expectations. The company has built and operated dozens of power plants throughout its 80-year history and is using that expertise to grow its competitive generation business without increasing risks.

Southern Company's competitive generation business is based on securing long-term contracts before any new power plants are added. That approach makes the company less vulnerable to the price volatility of the competitive wholesale electricity market. It sells primarily to regulated utilities and public power entities and only builds plants in the Southeast — the region it knows best.

The company's success is the result of this sound business strategy coupled with a deep commitment to the company's goals by nearly 26,000 talented, dedicated employees who work hard to ensure that customers have a reliable and affordable supply of electricity. They restore power quickly after a storm because customer service and satisfaction are what drive Southern Company's business.

GEORGIA POWER

Along with Southern Company's corporate office, Atlanta is home to four Southern Company subsidiaries, the largest being Georgia Power Company, which has a network of 15 generating plants and 20 hydroelectric dams that provide low-cost, reliable electricity for 2 million customers in all but six of the state's 159 counties.

Georgia Power's beginnings date back to 1883 during Atlanta's days as an emerging city recovering from the Civil War. That was the year Georgia Electric Light Company of Atlanta was formed and granted a franchise to install and energize the city's first electric street lights.

The company built its first generating plant the following year at Spring and Marietta streets and began providing service in 1885.

In 1891, banker Henry Atkinson gained control of the company and organized a new Georgia Electric Light Company. For more than 40 years thereafter, in conjunction with President Preston Arkwright, Atkinson led the company through rapid growth, expansion and dramatic changes. In 1926, with the merging of several power companies — including the original Atlanta utility company that had evolved into Georgia Railway and Power Company — Georgia Power Company was formed and joined Southeastern Power & Light, the holding company that preceded Southern Company.

In an address in 1927 to the National Electric Light Association in Atlantic City, Arkwright popularized the phrase, "A Citizen Wherever We Serve." To this day, it remains the core philosophy of Georgia Power, which now has nearly 8,800 employees throughout the state and serves customers in 57,000 of the state's 59,000 square miles.

The company provides excellent customer service — and has won numerous awards to back up that claim. Georgia Power maintains a reputation for superior reliability while keeping retail electric prices competitive.

The company is closely involved in many facets of the communities it serves, including civic and social efforts.

Georgia Power also has long played a major role in the economic development of Atlanta and the state. The company's economic development professionals help local communities marshal and direct resources to attract new business. The group is active in a number of efforts, including government and public-private partnerships to develop policies to expand and improve Georgia's economic, educational and environmental programs.

Georgia Power, which has been cited nationally for its economic development successes, played a major role in bringing the 1996 Olympics to Atlanta and providing infrastructure support as well as employee volunteer assistance during the event's run.

"Bringing new business, jobs and investments to Atlanta and Georgia is good for the company, the metro area and the state," says Mike Garrett, president of the company. "At Georgia Power, we work in partnership with government, business and education to help bring quality economic growth to communities across the state."

SOUTHERN LINC

Another Atlanta-based Southern Company subsidiary is Southern LINC. In business commercially since 1996, Southern LINC combines multiple communications options into one device, including two-way radio, phone service, one-way and two-way text messaging, wireless Internet access and wireless data access.

Southern Company originally designed the service to meet the needs of mobile businesses and provide Southern Company's five utility subsidiaries with reliable, wide-area wireless communications. The Southern LINC network was designed to remain up and running in extreme weather conditions, and every cell site on the network is monitored 24 hours a day, seven days a week. The wireless network covers 127,000 square miles in Atlanta and other major metro and rural areas in Georgia, Alabama, southeast Mississippi and northwest Florida.

Today Southern LINC has more than 260,000 customers that operate in virtually every industry, including service and sales, construction, emergency services, public safety, governmental services, forestry, public utilities and transportation.

SOUTHERN TELECOM

Southern Company's Southern Telecom subsidiary provides long-haul and metro dark fiber connecting Atlanta with other cities throughout the Southeast. The company is certified in Alabama, Florida, Texas and Georgia as well as at the federal level.

Southern Telecom has 1,300 route miles installed in the Southeast, including dark fiber routes from Atlanta to Jacksonville and Jacksonville to Miami, as well as a route up Florida's west coast through Tampa and Orlando and back to Daytona Beach. In the metro Atlanta area, Southern Telecom has completed an 11-mile optic ring serving all the premier carrier hotels and many enterprise buildings.

SOUTHERN COMPANY GAS

In the summer of 2002, Southern Company acquired the Georgia retail natural gas customers of NewPower. (Georgia is one of the few states with a competitive retail natural gas market.) Southern Company GAS provides natural gas service to residential, commercial and industrial customers located in Atlanta Gas Light's service territory.

With limited advertising, the company has seen improvement in its customer base and now has approximately 200,000 customers. The success of Southern Company GAS can be attributed to a strong and credible Southern Company brand presence in Georgia.

A BRIGHT FUTURE

Southern Company's strength is due in part to its success in coordinating specialized services between its companies — such as engineering, information technology, marketing and strategic planning.

Sharing engineering expertise and coordinating power supplies across the region, for example, has enabled Southern Company to operate its power plants at a 99 percent level of reliability and secure the most economical energy sources available. It also has allowed the company to keep reserve margins — the amount of generating capacity beyond what is needed to meet the projected peak demand for energy — at a level that provides a highly reliable supply of electricity to customers on even the hottest days of summer.

Southern Company achieves this while improving the environmental performance of its operations and pursuing ways to produce electricity more efficiently and cleanly than ever before. The company's goal is to have as little impact on the environment as possible while continuing to meet the region's growing energy needs.

Since 1990, Southern Company has reduced emissions of sulfur dioxide and nitrogen oxides combined by nearly 40 percent, while increasing energy output more than 30 percent. The company expects to invest more than $5 billion in additional environmental controls over the next decade to further reduce emissions.

Southern Company also is in partnership with others to research new technologies that generate energy with coal while producing dramatically fewer emissions or no emissions at all and is involved in stewardship efforts across the region. For example, Southern Company and the National Fish and Wildlife Foundation are initiating conservation projects for Southern birds in their natural habitats. Under the "Power of Flight" program, Southern Company will help implement bird habitat conservation efforts in Georgia, Florida, Alabama and Mississippi.

"I have a very positive feeling about the future of Southern Company and our strategy of sticking to what we do best," says CEO Ratcliffe. "We're going to continue focusing on customer satisfaction and on the nuts and bolts of running our business. And, of course, we're going to keep trying to do what's right and be a good citizen in the communities we serve."

Southern Company and its affiliates are active in the communities they serve across the Southeast. Employees participate in environmental stewardship and civic and social activities, including company-sponsored mentoring programs with area schoolchildren.

With steam, or water vapor, billowing from its massive cooling towers, Georgia Power's Plant Bowen is one of America's largest coal-fired generating facilities. Like all Southern Company coal-fired plants, it is equipped with electrostatic precipitators capable of removing up to 99.8 percent of particulate matter from emissions. Units at the plant, located north of Atlanta in Cartersville, also are equipped with selective catalytic reduction systems, which reduce emissions of nitrogen oxides by as much as 85 percent.

AGL Resources

1856... The tintype camera was patented. The Crimean War ended. James Buchanan was elected president. Booker T. Washington and Sigmund Freud were born. And Atlanta Gas Light lit the blue flame that would help to guide Georgia into the modern age.

Founded in 1856 to provide downtown Atlanta with 50 streetlights, Atlanta Gas Light is one of the nation's oldest utility companies. The same pioneering spirit that saw a role for the brand-new natural gas company at the beginning of the Industrial Age also has guided the formation of Atlanta Gas Light's parent company, AGL Resources, as an energy company for the future. The Atlanta-based company utilizes innovation, industry knowledge and strategically located assets to grow in a changing energy marketplace. AGL Resources provides service through five wholly owned subsidiaries and one partnership: gas distribution operations; retail gas marketing; natural gas asset optimization and asset management services; and telecommunications infrastructure services.

Through its businesses, AGL Resources serves more than 1.8 million customers in Georgia, Tennessee, Virginia, Texas and Arizona. In 2003 AGL Resources, traded on the New York Stock Exchange (NYSE: ATG), had revenues of $984 million and total assets of almost $4 billion.

A CHANGING INDUSTRY

The railroads made Georgia a transportation hub in the middle of the 19th century. When Atlanta Gas Light installed pipelines to bring natural gas to homes and businesses, Georgia was transformed into the industrial hub it is today. Natural gas also played an important role in the development of Georgia's municipalities as modern cities with lighted streets, heated homes, and commercial and residential growth — especially Atlanta. In 2003 Metro Atlanta's 10-county region contained almost 3.7 million residents, growing by 2.3 percent annually since the 2000 census.

Just as mode-of-travel has evolved from railroads to jets, bringing energy to a vastly increased population has changed as well. The energy industry has become infinitely more complex, yet the management of AGL Resources and Atlanta Gas Light has not only kept pace with industry changes, but has also anticipated them.

When deregulation of Georgia's natural gas industry occurred in 1997, Atlanta Gas Light became a distribution service, moving natural gas through its 35,200-mile pipeline system to homes and businesses in Georgia. With Atlanta Gas Light out of the gas sales business, AGL Resources formed a retailing subsidiary, SouthStar Energy Services, LLC. Operating as Georgia Natural Gas, it markets natural gas to approximately 550,000 customers in Georgia and 500 industrial customers in the Southeast.

BUSINESS INTEGRATION AND COORDINATION

The creation of Sequent Energy Management was an important step for the company — Sequent fills a niche in the energy market and has already produced value for ratepayers by leveraging AGL Resources assets to their advantage.

Another step toward this goal was taken with the creation of Sequent Energy Management to fill a niche in the energy market. As the "lean and mean" asset optimization arm of AGL Resources, Sequent focuses on asset optimization, producer services, wholesale marketing and risk management. The company, based in Houston, serves utilities, marketers, retail aggregators, municipalities and

AGL continues to implement new technologies to streamline its operations and improve the company's efficiency while serving 1.84 million residential and commercial gas customers in Georgia, Tennessee and Virginia.

large industrial customers primarily on the eastern half of the United States.

In 1856 there was no such thing as "telecommunications." Now telecommunication is considered to be as essential to modern life and business as traditional utility products like heat and water. AGL Resources' expertise in laying and maintaining gas pipelines naturally lends itself to construction and maintenance of telecommunications lines; AGL Networks was created to build fiber optic networks in metro Atlanta and has grown to serve Phoenix, Arizona, as well.

COMMUNITY SERVICE

Employees of AGL Resources and Atlanta Gas Light are as committed to helping their communities today as the founders of the company were almost 150 years ago. For example, in 2003 the Metro Atlanta Corporate Volunteer Council selected AGL Resources to receive its most prestigious honor, the IMPACT Award. Designed to foster corporate volunteerism, the IMPACT Award stands for Involvement Means People Acting in Communities Together. The award recognized the 33,000 volunteer hours given by employees in 2003 — activities that improved the lives of thousands of Atlantans.

The IMPACT Award and other recognitions are acknowledgement of the time, effort and funds that subsidiaries of AGL Resources put into their communities. In 2003 the company contributed $950,000 in funds and in-kind gifts for low-income energy assistance programs, economic development projects, leadership programs and other civic activities in Georgia, Tennessee, Texas and Virginia. Most weekends the AGL Resources V-Force teams of employees who volunteer their time are busy with projects ranging from building Habitat for Humanity houses, to working at local food banks, to mentoring teenagers. The company encourages employees to develop service projects that focus on three areas — education, community enrichment and environmental stewardship in order to make the most positive impact on their communities.

THE VALUE OF AGL RESOURCES

For Chairman, President and CEO Paula G. Rosput, "value" is key to the success of AGL Resources. From its retail and delivery services to efficient operation to community

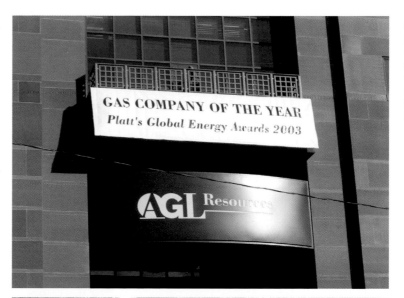

Citing superior financial performance and outstanding volunteer efforts, AGL Resources was named Best Gas Company in 2003 by Platts' Global Energy Awards.

Paula Rosput, AGL's chairman, president and CEO, unveils the Atlanta Gas Light/WSB Radio Shining Light Award in honor of the late Atlanta Mayor Maynard H. Jackson, Jr., as his wife Valerie and family members look on.

service, AGL Resources strives to give value to its customers, stockholders and communities.

"Flawless execution of our business, continued growth around existing assets, a strengthened financial base and creating a compelling demand for our services — each of these will add value to and strengthen our company," she said in a letter to shareholders. "We will continue to think smarter, work harder and contribute more to our shareholders, customers, communities and employees. Every day we're working hard to show you the real value is still here at AGL Resources."

Many things have changed since 1856. The pace of change will undoubtedly continue to quicken. But there are some reassuring constants found in a company with a proud history of service and value such as AGL Resources; constants like commitment to customers, dedication to community service, intense pride and a drive to keep providing value for its customers.

BellSouth Corporation

BellSouth has remained distinct from its counterparts in the communications industry through consistently recognized customer service and technologically advanced communications solutions. BellSouth's successes are reflections of a highly skilled, diverse workforce that is dedicated to its customers, the company and the communities it serves.

With help from employees like Retail Sales Consultant Leah Smith of Atlanta, Cingular Wireless added 745,000 net total cellular and PCS customers in third quarter 2003. It was the highest number of new customers in 10 quarters.

BellSouth is a Fortune 100 communications services company headquartered in Atlanta, Georgia, serving nearly 50 million local, long distance, Internet and wireless customers in the United States and 12 other countries. The company has 22 million equivalent access lines in the Southeastern United States and provides local residential and business service in nine states: Alabama, Florida, Georgia, Kentucky, Louisiana, Mississippi, North Carolina, South Carolina and Tennessee. BellSouth provides a full array of broadband data solutions to large, medium and small businesses. In the residential market, BellSouth offers DSL high-speed Internet access, advanced voice features and other services. BellSouth also offers long distance service throughout its markets, to both business and residential customers. The company's BellSouth Answers℠ packages combine local and long distance service with an array of

Services technician Tara Lapicola of Atlanta gets settled into her vehicle before her morning shift. BellSouth has won numerous awards for customer service, including a high ranking in the 2003 J.D. Power and Associates Local Residential Telephone Service.

calling features; wireless data, voice and e-mail services; high-speed DSL or dial-up Internet service; and wireless service. BellSouth also provides online and directory advertising services through BellSouth® RealPages.com℠ and The Real Yellow Pages®.

BellSouth owns 40 percent of Cingular® Wireless, the nation's second largest wireless company, through a joint venture with SBC Communications. Cingular provides innovative data and voice services and is the only U.S. wireless carrier to offer Rollover℠, the plan that allows customers to retain their unused monthly minutes.

Fortune has ranked BellSouth as "one of "America's Best Companies for Minorities" for five consecutive years.

BellSouth employees are dedicated to providing value through the company's community- and customer-first approach to doing business. With a workforce that reflects the diversity of the communities BellSouth serves, the company strives to deliver innovative products and services and to ensure that its communities become better places to live, work and grow. Guided by honesty and integrity, BellSouth aims to continue its longstanding tradition of excellence and remain the obvious choice for customers seeking high-value, high-quality data, voice and video communications services.

BellSouth has proven throughout the years to be a company committed to diversity and inclusion in the workplace. *Fortune* has ranked BellSouth as one of "America's Best Companies for Minorities" for five consecutive years. In addition, the NAACP has recognized BellSouth as an industry leader, ranking the company No.1 on its Telecommunications Industry Report Card since the report card inception in

1998. In 2003 BellSouth earned a position on DiversityInc.com's "Top Ten Companies for Executive Women." BellSouth offers a variety of networking groups open to all employees that focus attention on the interests of particular social, cultural, or other uniquely defined groups. Initiatives like BellSouth's diversity programs have aided in the development of a team-oriented approach to doing business.

BellSouth employees are recognized consistently for their commitment to customer service. Over the past decade, BellSouth has led its peer group in several survey honors including five years on *Fortune's* "Most Admired Company" listing. In 1999 BellSouth achieved its fourth-consecutive highest ranking in the J.D. Power and Associates Local Residential Telephone Service Satisfaction

Guided by honesty and integrity, BellSouth Corporation aims to continue its long-standing tradition of excellence and remain the obvious choice for customers seeking high-value, high-quality data, voice and video communications and services.

Study, which it achieved again in 2003. In addition, in its first full year as a provider of long distance service, BellSouth ranked fourth in customer satisfaction out of 17 long distance providers across the country, according to J.D. Power and Associates' 2003 Residential Long Distance Telephone Service Study. BellSouth also has won the

University of Michigan's American Customer Satisfaction Index the last 10 years running, giving the company a decade of distinction in customer service. The index is a uniform and independent measurement based on annual surveys of customers of more than 150 companies and 50 government agencies.

BellSouth employees' commitment to service continues into their retirement years. The BellSouth Pioneer Volunteers represent over 90,000 active and retired employees from throughout the BellSouth region. The Pioneers support a broad base of community programs centering on education, the environment, health, and human services and life enrichment. Over half of BellSouth's community outreach contributions come in the form of BellSouth Pioneer Volunteer service hours. Additional elements of the company's community initiatives include the BellSouth Foundation and BellSouth's charitable contributions program and corporate sponsorships. The BellSouth Foundation, an endowed trust with assets of approximately $50 million, focuses exclusively on education in BellSouth-served communities. Tradition and innovation will continue to be the lifeblood of BellSouth's culture, allowing the company to deliver service excellence to its customers and to proudly serve the communities in which it operates.

(Left and right) BellSouth has served as a long-standing partner with the American Red Cross (ARC) through participation in and organization of blood drives as well as disaster relief assistance. CEO Duane Ackerman (pictured left with Tim English, CEO-Metro Atlanta Chapter, American Red Cross) is among the many BellSouth supporters of the ARC. BellSouth collects thousands of pints of blood each year through blood drives in company buildings. In addition, BellSouth donated $1 million to the ARC to assist victims of the September 11 terrorist attacks.

(Left) BellSouth promotes its inclusion policies at a multicultural technology expo at the Georgia World Congress Center. The BellSouth Network of African American Telecommunications Professionals (BNAT) is one of six employee-networking groups supported by BellSouth's Office of Diversity.
(L to R) Monique Nero, Manager, Trade Shows and Events, Office of Diversity; Valencia Adams, Vice President and Chief Diversity Officer; Debbie Stone, Manager, Supplier Diversity and Ron Frieson, Vice President, Transition & Strategy, and former Chief Diversity Officer

Bennett International Group, Inc.

The history behind Atlanta-based Bennett International Group, Inc., makes a great story about how a small company can flourish into an industry leader with the right people behind the wheel.

Bennett is composed of several different companies that specialize in every aspect of transportation: Bennett Motor Express, Inc.-Freight; Bennett Motor Express-Drive Away; Bennett Express, Inc.; Bennett Truck Transport; Bennett Distribution Services; Bennett Network Systems; BDS Port Services; Bennett International Transport; Bennett Technology Group and Southern Thunder.

With worldwide service and thousands of clients scattered mostly throughout the United States and Canada, Bennett's start was rather small. In 1974, Marcia G. Taylor and her late husband, J.D. Garrison, purchased George Bennett Motor Express, which was a small contract carrier with only two customers and five trucks.

While working with just a handful of dedicated owner-operators, the company grossed over $1 million in revenues the following year. In 1978, the company purchased its first drop deck trailer. Two years later, it held its first annual agents meeting with only four agents. Later that same year, tragedy struck: Garrison suddenly fell ill and passed away.

Against all odds, Taylor kept the business alive and thriving. In the early 1980s, the company headed west to

Marcia Taylor, chief executive officer of Bennett International Group, Inc.

Ogden, Utah, where it opened a second office, then later built a 4,000-square-foot headquarters and repair facility in McDonough, Georgia.

The remainder of that decade was filled with smart business decisions and growth opportunities. The company introduced portable loading ramps, built a new 8,000-square-foot corporate headquarters adjacent to its existing building, established a travel agency called Transport Travel and began offering marshalling services, which ranged from inspecting imported goods for damage to warehousing and transporting them.

During the 1990s, the organization formed other companies, which handled ocean and airfreight and sold online supply chain management systems. Now it was beating its competitors in both service offerings and customer service. The once-small company had turned into a world-class operation.

Still, Bennett continued its climb to the top, setting higher service standards. In 1996, Bennett DriveAway was awarded the contract from the Atlanta Committee for the Summer Olympic Games to deliver 1,500 city buses from Transit Authorities throughout the country in just eight weeks. It completed the job in seven.

Along with new contracts and customers came a series of awards. Taylor, who served as the company's chief executive officer, and the company were formally recognized for their achievements. Ryder Carrier Management named the company Carrier of the Year in 1998 and Taylor was named female entrepreneur of the year in Georgia by *Venture* magazine. Then in 2003, Bennett was ranked No. 2 in the State of Georgia among the top women-owned companies in Atlanta.

The backbone of the Bennett family has always been its first company, Bennett Motor Express, Inc.-Freight, which supports three divisions: flatbed, drop deck/haul away and heavy haul.

The secret to Bennett's success is its people.

Each division offers a niche service with skilled operators and vehicles to match. In its flatbed division, qualified operators drive flatbed trucks with enough versatility and hauling power to safely deliver any cargo on time.

However, experienced drivers in its drop deck/haul away division use specially designed trailers with portable loading ramps that convert a drop deck into a haul away trailer when moving oversized equipment or wheeled vehicles. Likewise, trucks in its heavy haul fleet are well equipped with double-drop extendibles, detachable goosenecks and multi-axle trailers for oversized and overweight loads.

Another Bennett company — Bennett DriveAway — moves any type of single, driveaway rolling stock, such as cars, fire trucks, tractors, high-tech transit buses and motor coaches. All weigh thousands of pounds and some require special handling, such as cooling stops, fluid level checks and tire inspections. Whenever customers need to transport a large group of vehicles over a long distance, saddle mounting or decking is available, which usually saves customers thousands of dollars.

...in 2003, Bennett was ranked No. 2 in the State of Georgia among the top women-owned companies in Atlanta.

Since Bennett DriveAway supports offices in nearly every major port city in the United States, it works closely with Bennett International Transport to ship products overseas. Customers receive one bill for all their moving expenses such as coordinating ocean freight or insurance and international banking services.

If it rolls or can be lifted, Bennett will find a safe way to move it. That goes for houses, too. Bennett Truck Transport

moves manufactured homes, modular buildings, commercial office units, multi-section homes, repos and singlewide sections that range up to 18-feet wide and 120-feet long.

...Taylor was named female entrepreneur of the year in Georgia by *Venture* magazine.

Part of Bennett's success is due to independent owner-operators. The company leases its services because of its professional abilities, years of safe driving experience and willingness to undertake and accomplish any task.

Whenever any of the company's agents secure freight from customers, Bennett Network Systems kicks in. Brokerage staff locates the appropriate truck and equipment to haul the load, schedule pick-ups and follow through with customers to ensure their freight is delivered on time.

Other value-added services are offered by Bennett Distribution Services, such as inspections, warehousing and storage, packaging, loading and unit and product tracking, which relies on Web-based technology supported by the Bennett Technology Group (BTG).

Online software created by BTG helps customers gain visibility to their entire supply chain, access any information about their shipment at any time and generate status reports on demand. Its consultants also help clients design effective and efficient supply chain business processes.

Despite all that Bennett offers, the company still found another way to service customers. In 1996, it opened a retail store, called Sudden Thunder, or better known as Easyriders of Atlanta, which specializes in the sale and service of Harley Davidson and Big Dog motorcycles.

There's no telling what Bennett may accomplish next. Based on its corporate philosophy of delivering top-quality services, the company will continue leading the transportation industry as North America's highway to the world.

PS Energy Group, Inc.

From a start-up business run from the basement of President and CEO Livia Whisenhunt's home to the $100-million company it is today, Atlanta-based PS Energy Group credits much of its success to the city's active promotion of the entrepreneurial spirit coupled with the firm and visionary leadership of its founder. Renowned for

its stellar customer service and its unsurpassed problem-solving abilities, the company currently offers a full range of energy products for production and transportation including natural gas and propane, as well as providing diesel fuel and gasoline to industrial and commercial customers. Although PS Energy has grown to market its products and services nationwide, its strong commitment to local Atlanta markets is reflected in more than 60 percent of its revenues being in its home market, contributing significantly to the standard of living in the city that has enabled the company to thrive.

Shortly after its founding in 1985 as a marketer of bulk transportation fuels — primarily gasoline and diesel fuels — PS Energy added natural gas to the types of fuels it marketed and emerged as one of the first companies to market gas behind the Atlanta Gas Light (AGL) system when deregulation to the city gate occurred. In 1990 PS Energy acquired 100-percent ownership of The Gas Key Corporation, then an unattended fueling business. In 1998 it became a certified natural gas provider through which PS Energy supplies natural gas to residential and commercial customers in Georgia. More than a decade of

experience and expertise enables PS Energy Group to provide a competitively priced variety of services designed to meet specific requirements including nomination and balancing management.

Along with natural gas PS Energy has continued to add numerous other products and services to its diverse array of offerings. The company's well-known Fuel Management Program evolved from the company's bulk fuel expertise and the acquisition of Unattended Fuel Outlets (UFO's) in 1989. Since the mid-90s, the company has acquired major fuel management contracts while expanding its services to include emergency fueling services as well as value-added services such as inventory management, computerized monitoring and control of customer- owned fueling stations, unattended fuel outlets, and the universal purchase cards, which combine the data from fuel dispensed onsite with data from retail fuel purchases. Relatively recent additions to PS Energy's range of products and services include global positioning and vehicle tracking, a fully integrated solution allowing for uncomplicated management of an enterprise's work processes, mobile work force and assets, including total fleet management and dispatching services for fleets of any type or size. Always looking to the future, PS Energy is already a registered electricity marketer in the state of Georgia, and the company is positioned to actively market electricity nationally as the deregulation in that industry stabilizes. This wide range of products and services provides PS Energy a distinct competitive advantage among larger and similarly sized energy merchant companies nationwide.

Both residents and visitors to Atlanta enjoy and benefit from the positive impact PS Energy Group's forward-looking products and services bring to the Atlanta area on a daily basis. The company has a number of multiyear fuel management contracts in a variety of stages with clients such as The Southern Company (Georgia Power and Alabama Power), Texas Utilities, XCEL Energy and a number of government agencies including local school districts. Additionally both residents and visitors to Atlanta reaped the benefits of PS Energy Group's fuel management expertise during the 1996 Summer Olympics, when ACOG and MARTA awarded PS Energy a contract to build and manage temporary fueling sites for transit buses brought in to accommodate increased transportation needs. PS Energy's emergency services provide substation fueling and mobile fueling for utility crews during power outages in nine southeastern states.

PS Energy Group's unmatched ability to provide an extensive array of fuel management products and services coupled with its sterling customer service record have led to numerous awards and recognitions throughout the company's existence. Early on the YWCA recognized PS Energy Group with its 1991 PROWESS award (Program for Women's Empowerment, Skills and Success) for small business. The company has since received the prestigious Administrator's Award for Excellence from the United States Small Business Administration in four separate years. In 1997 the company won the "Hammer Award" from Vice President Gore's National Performance Review Board. PS Energy Group ranked number 139 in *Working Woman Magazine*'s top 500 woman-owned businesses in 2001. Two years later the company ranked number 46 in *Hispanic Business Magazine*'s top 500 Hispanic-owned businesses and was ranked third in the state of Georgia for minority-owned companies.

Such prestigious accomplishments by PS Energy Group have come about largely due to the visionary leadership of the woman who has been at the helm since the very beginning, President and CEO Livia Whisenhunt. Her expertise and skills in the energy marketing industry were widely recognized and prompted her appointment to the state of Georgia Joint House-Senate Competitive Natural Gas Service Study Committee in 1996. Likewise, her knowledge gained her appointment to the Southeastern Region Federal Regulatory Fairness Board (REGFAIR) in 1999. She later was appointed the REGFAIR Region IV Chairperson. Demonstrating a commitment to Atlanta, Ms. Whisenhunt represented PS Energy Group on the Carter Center's board of councilors and on the board of directors for Zoo Atlanta during which time PS Energy's donations helped make Zoo Atlanta a renowned zoological park.

Ms. Whisenhunt was a founding member and PS Energy one of the founding supporters of Camp Twin Lakes, a camping facility in metro Atlanta for children with special needs. PS Energy's multi-faceted community involvement has also included support for several local school sports and science programs.

Guided by the visionary leadership of such a strong and forward-looking president and CEO, PS Energy Group has grown into one of the most important companies of its kind, locally, regionally and nationally. Core values including integrity, fostering customer loyalty through impeccable service, prompt vendor payments and outstanding employee benefits perfectly complement PS Energy Group's remarkable "just do it" attitude, which allows the company to regularly and fearlessly accomplish tasks that would daunt a company many times its size. Add to this a focus on commitment to excellence in responsiveness to customer needs and customer service and an ability to recognize and embrace opportunities to develop new products and services, and it's understandable why PS Energy Group continues to flourish both within Atlanta and beyond.

"Atlanta has always been willing to look beyond its borders. This willingness has inspired, among other things, an international transportation hub, centers of higher education and research unsurpassed in their excellence, as well as diversity and cultural organizations recognized throughout the world for their achievement. Sutherland is proud to have played a small part in the development of these institutions and grateful to have benefited from Atlanta's vibrant business environment."

Jim Henderson, Managing Partner
Sutherland Asbill & Brennan LLP

"Atlanta has become the third largest home to Fortune 100 companies. It has created over a million new jobs in approximately the last decade. We have grown with the City and clients like The Coca-Cola Company, UPS, The Home Depot, SunTrust Banks, Georgia Pacific and Scientific-Atlanta as Atlanta has become a crossroads for international business and a cultural hub for the Southeast."

Walter W. Driver, Jr, Chairman
King & Spalding LLP

PROFESSIONAL SERVICES

Atlanta offers premier professional services that meet even the most complex needs of the city's businesses and residents.

Bennett Thrasher PC

A premier provider of professional financial services, Bennett Thrasher is one of the largest accounting and consulting firms in Atlanta. The firm's overriding objective is providing timely, high-quality audit, accounting, tax, and consulting services to clients in the best professional manner.

> ## The firm's overriding objective is providing timely, high-quality audit, accounting, tax, and consulting services to clients in the best professional manner.

Since its inception in 1980, Bennett Thrasher's commitment to its core values remains the bedrock of its success. Customer service, employee fellowship, community involvement, growth and prosperity-its own, and those it serves-are the hallmarks that define the achievements of the firm. Bennett Thrasher places the greatest importance on its integrity, and takes a profound interest in its clients, their financial needs, and sustained success.

Bennett Thrasher is firmly committed to client satisfaction, and the financial professionals at the firm have the experience, education, and dedication to deliver the highest standard of expertise to their most important commodity: their clients. Each specialist at the firm realizes that timeliness is of utmost value, directly affecting everyone's bottom line. The commitments made by the employees at Bennett Thrasher to their clients and associates are promises on which they intend to deliver to the best of their abilities, as quickly as possible, resulting in a shared success enjoyed by all parties.

> ## Customer service, employee fellowship, community involvement, growth and prosperity-its own, and those it serves-are the hallmarks that define the achievements of the firm. Bennett Thrasher places the greatest importance on its integrity, and takes a profound interest in its clients, their financial needs, and sustained success.

Co-founding Shareholder, Kenneth L. Thrasher

Each shareholder at Bennett Thrasher brings a high level of achievement and experience to his or her work. Founding shareholders Richard Bennett and Kenneth Thrasher share extensive experience. Their diverse and far-reaching experiences include expertise in mergers, acquisitions, business consulting; corporate, partnership, and individual income tax planning; real estate development, construction contracting, equipment sales and leasing; printing and paper manufacturing; and hospitality and service industries. Both Rick and Ken hold advanced degrees in their field, and the presence of both gentlemen is strong in the Atlanta community.

The men and women who make up Bennett Thrasher share a common commitment to quality, integrity, client service, and professionalism.

Although Bennett Thrasher is an Atlanta-based firm, the list of services it offers rivals that of any national group. From the requisite income tax planning and preparation to the most in-depth business valuation and complicated sales and mergers, Bennett Thrasher's team has a deep bench of leading associates capable of accomplishing any task set before them. In addition to the numerous financial services available, Bennett Thrasher offers a long list of complimentary services including: litigation support services, consultative and contract accounting services, expert witness services, estate and retirement planning, fraud prevention and detection, state and local tax consulting, business consulting, and more.

Bennett Thrasher Values Statement

INTEGRITY
We are who we say we are: we do what we say we will do.

FAMILY
We support the family as the primary institution of society.

CLIENTS
We serve our clients. We meet their needs.

Through an affiliation with DFK International, a worldwide association of independent accounting firms and business advisors, Bennett Thrasher has the ability to service clients locally, throughout the United States, and abroad. DFK International, founded in 1962, is now one of the world's major international networks of independent accountancy firms and business advisors.

Founding shareholders Richard Bennett and Kenneth Thrasher share extensive experience. Their diverse and far-reaching experiences include expertise in mergers, acquisitions, business consulting; corporate, partnership, and individual income tax planning; real estate development, construction contracting, equipment sales and leasing; printing and paper manufacturing; and hospitality and service industries.

The men and women who make up Bennett Thrasher share a common commitment to quality, integrity, client service, and professionalism. This commitment, partnered with the vast experience of its employees and wide array of services offered, defines Bennett Thrasher as a leader of its industry in Atlanta.

Co-founding Shareholder, Richard A. Bennett

King & Spalding LLP

"There's no *better way to live than being a lawyer. Your have a chance to serve, you have a chance to use your talents, and all in the public good."*

This sentiment, voiced by former U.S. Attorney General and King & Spalding LLP retired partner Griffin Bell, states the philosophy of Atlanta's premier law firm, including its mission to serve clients and community.

In 1885, just 20 years after the flames of the American Civil War left much of the South in ashes, Alexander Campbell King and Jack Johnson Spalding formed a legal partnership in Atlanta. Since that time, the partnership has expanded into an internationally respected firm with additional offices in Houston, Washington, D.C., New York and London. Much of the firm's spectacular growth has paralleled the international expansion and increasingly complex legal needs of its clients, many of which are also headquartered in Atlanta, including The Coca-Cola Company, SunTrust Banks, Inc., UPS and The Home Depot®.

An example of this parallel growth is exhibited in one of King & Spalding's first and most important client partnerships, The Coca-Cola Company. The relationship was forged in the 1920s, when King & Spalding executed a merger between Coca-Cola and its bottling company. The firm has since been intimately involved in Coca-Cola's growth, consistently rising to the unique challenges as Coca-Cola grew from a fledgling company to the most recognized brand in the world. King & Spalding has worked with Coca-Cola on everything from legislative policy to acquisitions to litigation. The firm also assisted former Coca-Cola CEO Robert Woodruff with the incorporation of his family's many foundations. In 1979 the law firm opened its first out-of-state office in Washington D.C. and began to assist Coca-Cola in addressing its growing legislative and regulatory matters.

Atlanta's reputation as a business capital was partially secured in the 1920s, when then-senior partner Hughes Spalding launched a public and private campaign to alter inhospitable state tax laws that had forced Coca-Cola to move its corporate headquarters to Delaware. As former governor, Ellis Arnall, once noted: "What is good for Coke is good for Georgia." As a result of Spalding's and the firm's efforts, the laws were changed and Coca-Cola's corporate headquarters, as well as many thousands of others in the following decades, moved to Atlanta.

King & Spalding's successful reputation as an advocate for businesses of all sizes has attracted hundreds of new clients through the years. One such thriving entrepreneurial endeavor that became a significant client is The Home Depot®. Founded in Atlanta in 1978, The Home Depot® has become the world's largest home improvement specialty retailer and the second-largest retailer in the United States. The retailer will soon open its 1,800th store in 50 states, the District of Columbia, Puerto Rico, eight Canadian provinces and Mexico. King & Spalding has been there throughout its expansion to serve many of its growing legal needs. For example, when King & Spalding opened its Houston office, the firm hired several outstanding Spanish-speaking attorneys to handle significant transactional work in Latin America for The Home Depot® and for major energy clients, such as ChevronTexaco Corp. and Shell Oil.

Throughout its history, King & Spalding has carefully nurtured its outstanding reputation through a simple

(Opposite page top) Mason W. Stephenson, Managing Partner of the Atlanta office; Lovita T. Tandy, Partner; and C. William Baxley, Partner.

Chilton D. Varner, Partner; Thomas B. Gaines, Jr., Partner and Chief Information Officer; and Walter W. Driver, Jr., Chairman of the Firm.

(Opposite page bottom) King & Spalding volunteers have helped construct six homes for Atlanta Habitat for Humanity.

King & Spalding's success has always been based on a strong commitment to public service, and the firm has encouraged its partners accordingly. Its partners and associates have a heritage of strong moral and judicious qualities. As a result, its lawyers have been selected for many prestigious positions, including Attorney General, Deputy Attorney General, Solicitor General and Deputy Solicitor General of the United States of America. Other partners have previously served as Governor and U.S. Senator.

Since its humble beginnings as a two-person firm, King & Spalding has expanded considerably and now comprises nearly 800 lawyers and offices in Atlanta, Houston, London, New York and Washington, D.C. King & Spalding currently represents 250 public companies, including more than half of the *Fortune* 100 companies. The firm negotiates and executes transactions of all types across Europe and South America and tries lawsuits in virtually every state, continuing to shape the companies and communities it touches through a firm knowledge of the law and a strong dedication to its community.

formula of providing the best advice and service to its clients. The firm ensures this tradition by hiring men and women who have the finest legal minds, have excelled in their education and who exercise superb judgment. While all of the attorneys at King & Spalding can boast of individual achievements, perhaps the firm's strongest attribute is its ability to put together an outstanding team to manage complicated matters for the benefit of its clients. Founder Jack Spalding's farsighted words, "No one member can make as much individual reputation in any other way than by building the firm," still hold true today.

In addition to its many corporate achievements, King & Spalding has been steadfastly dedicated to the development of Atlanta and the region through civic and political involvement. From the firm's efforts to effectively improve state legislation to spur corporate growth, to its early involvement in the city's efforts to secure the 1996 Centennial Olympic Games, to its present support of quality-of-life initiatives such as the Metro Atlanta Task Force for the Homeless and the Atlanta Clean Air Campaign, King & Spalding has proven to be a leader in all phases of civic life.

Included in King & Spalding's list of community contributions is its determination to go above and beyond the call of duty through its commitment to *pro bono* work. Lawyers have eagerly volunteered their time in civic, criminal and legislative projects around the country. Consequently, in 2003 the Georgia Bar Association and the Washington Lawyers' Committee for Civil Rights and Urban Affairs honored King & Spalding by presenting the firm with the organizations' most prestigious pro bono achievement awards.

Corporate Facilities Group, Inc.

Corporate Facilities Group, Inc., as its name suggests, is an Atlanta-based company that handles facilities management for a full spectrum of business — commercial, retail, medical, aviation, industrial, government, high- and mid-rise buildings — and is currently expanding its medical and office market management. Bob Gillespie established facilities Engineering in 1995 and formed the patent company, Corporate Facilities Group Inc., in 2000. Corporate Facilities Group, Inc. also operates Condominium Management Group, Inc. of Florida and performs shopping mall maintenance and facilities management in Brazil.

CFG's Vice President Bud Herring (Left) and President Bob Gillespie (Right)

Gillespie's experiences growing up on a large Pennsylvania hog farm and service in the U.S. Navy offered him valuable insight into team efforts. When he formed Facilities Engineering he wanted a business associate he could trust implicitly, one who thought similarly to Gillespie. He remembered James "Bud" Herring, who had worked for Gillespie in the early 90s, and brought him into the operation.

Gillespie and Herring knew that most condominium management companies didn't pay employees well, resulting in continual turnover, so they deliberately geared Corporate Facilities Group (CFG) to operate with a different twist and formed Condominium Management Group, Inc. — to find great maintenance technicians and offer them great compensation and benefits. Gillespie and Herring decided to reduce their management fees in order to pump income into employee compensation. By focusing on employees, employees can concentrate on CFG customers — a company slogan puts it, "We work from our hearts first and our wallets last" — and CFG provides its employees with highly focused technical, life safety and hazardous materials training as well as training for compliance with OSHA regulations.

"We work from our hearts first and our wallets last."

Gillespie and Herring also established three business goals: to raise the bar of service of excellence through superior customer service; increase the value of customers' assets through comprehensive preventive maintenance; and reduce customers' expenses through comprehensive energy management and costs reduction programs, national purchasing of goods and services, and comprehensive, clearly defined specifications for contracted services.

CFG manages over 18 million square feet of real estate and has never lost a client in its eight years of operation. Major clients include Home Depot corporate headquarters, Kaiser Permanente hospitals, General Electric, Veterans Affairs' regional office and Delta Airlines. CFG is strictly a facilities management and technical consulting services firm, unconcerned with property leasing and brokerage. It operates facilities with a high focus on energy management, national vendor partnerships to reduce operating expenses, and quality facility management operations.

Today CFG not only retains approximately 85 dedicated employees but also has experienced phenomenal growth — 30 percent in 2002 alone, along with considerable additional growth in 2003. Because CFG's profit margins aren't as high as those of brokerage and leasing companies, and it isn't laden with corporate bureaucracy, it can offer an excellent product at much lower costs. These factors have led it to be called "the Charles Schwab of facilities management." CFG's track record of phenomenal growth and an increasing number of satisfied clients clearly indicate it has earned this handsome sobriquet.

Heidrick & Struggles

Fifty Years of Service Excellence: Heidrick & Struggles Marks a Milestone

It all began with a handshake. In 1953, Gardner Heidrick and John Struggles teamed up to form a new kind of professional services firm, one that would identify and recruit top-level managers for Midwestern manufacturing and commercial companies. It was an untested, even radical, idea and there was no assurance of success. The two men

> ### The firm provides service to the Southeast market, with representation in both Atlanta and Jacksonville, Florida.

sealed their new partnership in an office in Chicago, little knowing that they were embarking on the industry known today as executive search — an industry based on the management of human capital.

Fifty years later, Heidrick & Struggles International, Inc. has evolved into a global network of professionals dedicated to the belief that human capital is the world economy's most valuable resource. Inevitably, the firm's structure and operations have grown more complex and multifaceted. But amid all the changes, Heidrick & Struggles continues to steer by the same values that guided its founders. It's an ethic that, in the words of the firm's honored Partnership Spirit statement, "places the interests of our clients, our firm and our colleagues above our own." Heidrick & Struggle's commitment to quality, client service, partnership, integrity, and the drive for excellence is as strong today as it was when Gardner Heidrick and John Struggles shook hands in that Chicago office 50 years ago.

From its position as the premier executive search and leadership services firm for thousands of organizations around the globe, it can see that the need for effective leadership will only intensify in future years. Boards of directors and chief executives today face the challenging task of creating an environment in which people want to, and can, perform at the highest levels of their potential.

A contributing member of the business community since 1980, the Atlanta office of Heidrick & Struggles serves client organizations as trusted advisors, partnering

with them to attract, retain and nurture the best talent in today's ever-changing business environment. The firm provides service to the Southeast market, with representation in both Atlanta and Jacksonville, Florida.

To serve the broader leadership requirements of clients, the firm has developed other leadership solutions to complement its core executive search business, including executive assessment, interim executive placement and professional development. Combining these services with a greater focus on major account development enables Heidrick & Struggles to build deep and lasting relationships with its clients.

The strategic use of human capital is equally or even more critical as a sustainable and additive competitive advantage than technology, a global presence, a strong balance sheet, or physical assets. Indeed, the companies that will thrive in the years ahead are those that invest in

Back row, left to right: J. Rucker McCarty, Senior Partner; Charles E. Commander, IV, Partner; Ellen E. Brown, Principal; and M. Evan Lindsay, Senior Partner. Front row, left to right: Jane M. Stevenson, Senior Partner and Dale E. Jones, Managing Partner.

recruiting high-impact people, in assessing leadership potential of executives, in developing talent to its fullest and in retaining employees for the long haul.

As Heidrick & Struggles International, Inc. celebrates its 50-year milestone and looks ahead to the next half century, it gladly acknowledges the source of its success: a company-wide commitment to enduring values because that is what will continue to guide the firm into the future.

Assessing, acquiring, developing, and retaining top people are its competencies. Heidricks & Struggles invites clients to make them theirs.

Peachtree's mission includes "carrying God's love to the world." Through our involvement with more than 30 community ministry partners in the Atlanta area, and through global mission partnerships in 13 countries on five continents, we send God's love around the corner and around the world every day.

Rev. Marnie M. Crumpler, Executive Pastor
Peachtree Presbyterian Church

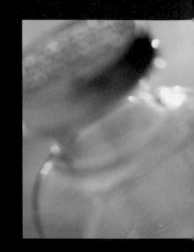

QUALITY OF LIFE

A diverse collection of services and organizations contribute to the health and well-being of residents and visitors, providing countless benefits and opportunities that help define the Atlanta lifestyle.

The Carter Center

FIGHTING DIS-
EASE, AND BUILDING HOPE: In the United States and in
countries across the globe, The Carter Center reaches out
to leaders at the highest levels of government and to vil-
lagers in the poorest areas of the world to carry out its mission. Established by former U.S. President Jimmy Carter
and his wife, Rosalynn, in 1982 in partnership with Emory
University, the Center has helped to improve life for people
in more than 65 nations.

those early years. Today we address the root causes of
conflict as well — the need for adequate food, access to
health care, freedom, economic opportunity, and democracy.
All of these are basic human rights."

Since its inception, The Carter Center has brought
together diverse people and groups to work toward these
common goals with exceptional results. The Center has
observed more than 50 elections to help strengthen
democracies in Asia, Latin America, and Africa; helped

(Left)
A woman in a village in
Ghana strains her
family's water through a
nylon filter to prevent
them from contracting
Guinea worm disease.
E. Howard

(Right)
In negotiations
guided by The Carter
Center, Sudan and
Uganda signed an
agreement in 1999
to resume
diplomatic relations.
The Carter Center

ADVANCING HUMAN RIGHTS

The nonpartisan and not-for-profit organization was
formed just one year after the end of Carter's 1977-1981
term as president. "We envisioned that The Carter Center
would be a place like Camp David, where parties in conflict could come to resolve their differences," said President
Carter. "But it has grown far beyond what we imagined in

farmers double or triple grain production in 15 African
countries; mediated or worked to prevent civil and
international conflicts; intervened to prevent unnecessary
diseases in Latin America and Africa, including the near
eradication of Guinea worm disease; and strived to diminish
the stigma against people with mental illness. The visible
impact of this work was cited by the Norwegian committee
that awarded President Carter the Nobel Peace Prize in 2002.

CHANGING LIVES

Focusing on challenges in peace and health, the Center
takes an action-oriented approach, applying academic
research to on-the-ground projects with clear promise to
advance human rights and alleviate human suffering.
Although the Center has hosted many high-level conferences on important global issues, a requirement is that all
such meetings result in action plans leading to results.

"By sharing with people the tools and knowledge they
need to address their own problems and take ownership
for them, we build capacity within communities and

Former U.S. President
Jimmy Carter was
awarded the Nobel
Peace Prize in
Oslo, Norway,
on December 10, 2002,
for "his decades of
untiring effort to find
peaceful solutions to
international conflicts,
to advance democracy
and human rights,
and to promote
economic and
social development."
Knudsen's Fotosenter

Located in a 35-acre park, the Center overlooks Atlanta's skyline. The Carter Presidential Center complex includes the not-for-profit Carter Center and the Jimmy Carter Library and Museum, owned and operated by the National Archives and Records Administration of the federal government. Open to the public are the museum and grounds, including Japanese and other gardens, natural wooded areas, ponds, and a meadow. The Carter Center Web site provides a wealth of additional information on the Center and its activities.

Photos courtesy The Georgia High Program

nations to achieve and sustain progress against complex and interrelated challenges in peace and health," said Deanna Congileo, Carter Center spokesperson.

A notable example is the campaign to eradicate Guinea worm disease, an ancient and horrible parasitic disease that has afflicted 17 countries in Africa and three in Asia. Guinea worm transmission has been reduced by 99 percent, from 3.5 million cases in 1986 to fewer than 23,000 reported in 2004, through an international coalition led by The Carter Center. By training village volunteers to teach their neighbors simple preventive measures, such as filtering drinking water to strain out the worm larvae and keeping infected people from entering public water sources, the Center has stimulated development of a self-sustaining infrastructure for health care education and delivery in tens of thousands of communities abroad. Now, the Center is applying this public health model to other diseases, including lymphatic filariasis (elephantiasis), schistosomiasis, river blindness, and trachoma.

PIONEERING PEACE

The Center also promotes peace in troubled areas around the world. Known for brokering the historic Camp David peace accords between Egypt and Israel in 1978, the former President and his staff have addressed conflicts in Haiti, North Korea, Bosnia, Sudan, Uganda, Liberia, and other nations. A pioneer in international election observation, the Center has promoted elections as another route to conflict resolution, giving millions of people worldwide a new voice in how they are governed. Since 1989, the Center has sent monitors to assess election processes in emerging democracies throughout Latin America, Africa, and Asia.

Also addressed are "second-generation democracy issues," such as strengthening institutions to safeguard citizens' rights, increasing the role of citizens in public policy formation, and discouraging corruption through government transparency and accountability. Realizing that people's faith in democracy and a country's chances for peace are bolstered by adequate economic opportunity, the Center also helps countries craft comprehensive strategies for economic and social development, focusing on the need to include people from all sectors of society in planning a nation's future.

Said President Carter during his Nobel Peace Prize Lecture, "We can choose to alleviate suffering. We can choose to work together for peace. We can make these changes — and we must."

Mt. Bethel United Methodist Church

More than 160 years ago, a handful of Christian settlers in Marietta laid the groundwork for what has grown into one of the region's most dynamic churches, committed to involvement in its community through worship, opportunities for fellowship, and service.

In 1840 Bethel Methodist Episcopal Church was organized by 13 charter members on the north side of Lower Roswell Road, about one-half mile east of Johnson Ferry Road. In 1870 John Hayes donated two acres of land where members built the one-room church that is now Mt. Bethel's historic chapel. Mt. Bethel, meaning "House of God," became the new name of the church, later renamed Mt. Bethel United Methodist Church. Today, with 7,800 members, two traditional worship services, a blended service, and one contemporary service, Mt. Bethel UMC is both one of the fastest-growing churches in the region and of United Methodist churches in the country.

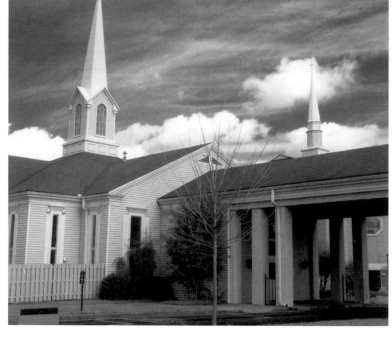

Mt. Bethel's membership voted to keep both steeples when the new sanctuary (rear) was built in 1996.
Photo by Pam Moxley

The first expansion of the church occurred in August 1950, when three rooms were added to the one-room building for Sunday school classes, along with a small porch at the building front. The following decades witnessed phenomenal growth. Three additional classrooms and a hall were added in 1956; a parsonage was purchased in 1966; eight acres of land on Lower Roswell Road — about one mile west of Johnson Ferry Road — were bought for a new site in 1969; and the church building was moved in February 1972. Membership was under 200 in 1972, but doubled to 450 by 1978 and continued to double every five years — to 913 by January 1983, to 1,852 by January 1988, and to 3,647 in 1993.

More than 300 campers and volunteers attended Camp Hope® in 2004, a week-long camp for children whose parents are in Georgia prisons. Mt. Bethel was the first church to back Camp Hope® in 2000, and continues to provide strong support.

Ministries of the church kept pace as the affluent, family-oriented East Cobb County area grew. Accordingly, a new sanctuary and educational building were built and consecrated in 1985; a 43,000-square-foot Christian Activity Center opened in 1990; and adjoining land to the church site was purchased in 1992 for future growth. A visioning process in 1994 revealed that the church was called to expand Christ's kingdom by continuing to accommodate growth. The following year a third worship service was added to help relieve the overcrowded conditions and Mt. Bethel began televising Sunday services as an outreach to the 60 percent un-churched local population.

In 1996 the church approved a multimillion-dollar, six-year campaign for a new 2,000-seat sanctuary — the church's fourth — and renovation of the existing sanctuary into a two-story, education building that now accommodates adult Sunday school classes and Bible studies.

That long-range vision also included a new education facility for the 654 students who attend the Christian Academy, which offers an academically excellent, Christ-centered education for children in kindergarten through eighth grade. The 36-classroom building also accommodates all children's Sunday school classes, children's worship and special Bible studies for children.

East Cobb's family-heavy demographics influenced the planning of the new Christian Activities Center, which opened in 2003 and contains a full-court gym, indoor track, climbing wall, full workout facilities and concession stand. The church's 44-acre campus also encompasses playing fields for youth and adult soccer, softball and baseball, attracting more than 1,000 children — many of

The one-room 1870 Mt. Bethel church is the present chapel on Mt. Bethel's church site.

whom are non-members — to Mt. Bethel recreational programs each season. Those same demographics also keep Mt. Bethel's pre-school program full — for more than 20 years, the Christian Academy Preschool has nurtured 400 toddlers and children each year. In addition, Mt. Bethel provides day care to 90 children each day with one of the few church-owned day care centers in the area.

Celebrating God through the gift of music is a high priority at Mt. Bethel; programs offer many avenues for celebration through adult, youth and children's choirs, hand bell choirs, orchestra, brass ensemble, praise bands and more. A concert-quality choir, a concert-quality pipe organ and talented organists combine to present concerts regularly.

The Women's Ministry at Mt. Bethel exists to embrace women of all ages and stages, and to teach, empower, support and guide them in their growth as women of God. This ministry includes the popular Ladies' Nights Out and an annual winter Women's Retreat.

Reaching out to the community is a central portion of Mt. Bethel's mission. With one of the few such church-supported programs in the area, the Older Adult Day Center offers a weekday program for any older adult in the community who is seeking a structured social environment, or whose caregiver seeks respite care for adults who have memory impairments. The church also coordinates a family caregiver support group and evenings out opportunities. Mt. Bethel Shepherd Center Counseling and Life Ministries provides counseling, family and life education, support and spiritual growth services to the members of Mt. Bethel and the local community.

In addition to these ministries, the church offers an annual marriage retreat, and short-term

mission trips to Central America, South America and Eastern Europe for those seeking to grow spiritually and share their talents. The Stephen Ministry of trained lay persons reaches out to help others during times of loss, divorce, death, illness, family problems and career issues. The annual Great Day of Service deploys a thousand church members into the community who tackle one-day fix-up projects for local charitable agencies, underprivileged churches and schools, and shut-ins. Since 1999 Mt. Bethel has sponsored a benefit concert for Camp Hope®, a weeklong summer camp for fourth- and fifth-grade children of inmates in Georgia's prison system — a ministry endorsed by the state of Georgia. And since 1992 Mt. Bethel UMC has built 19 Habitat for Humanity homes, recently committing to funding and constructing two homes per year for needy families in Cobb County.

Church members are proud of their enthusiasm, wide variety of ministries and activities, commitment and outreach to the community, and beautiful church campus, and always welcome anyone who may be seeking a church home that is not just a building, but is the sum of interesting people and loving hearts that gives Mt. Bethel UMC its soul.

Adjacent to the new sanctuary is Lauren's Garden, dedicated to the memories of children who have passed away.
Photo by Pam Moxley

Peachtree Presbyterian Church

Since its founding in 1919 Peachtree Presbyterian Church, located in the heart of Buckhead in Atlanta, Georgia, has grown into a community of more than 9,000 members devoted to worshiping, growing and giving in the name of Jesus Christ. Led by senior pastor Dr. Victor Pentz, Peachtree Presbyterian offers not only five Sunday services each week, but also numerous additional programs and services, from educational and supportive peer groups to local and global mission opportunities, counseling services, a child development center and preschool, a recreation center and more — all operated as a reflection of the church's mission.

Peachtree Presbyterian Church

Peachtree's mission embraces the New Testament model of the church. Arranged around an appropriate acronym — P.E.A.C.H. — this mission is as follows: Proclaim Christ and membership in His family (evangelism); Enjoy growing in God's Word (discipleship); Adventure into serving one another (pastoral care); Carry God's love to the world (mission); and Honor God with all that we are (worship). As Peachtree wants its members to grow as disciples of Jesus Christ, so does it enlist their assistance in fulfilling its mission.

Dr. Victor D. Pentz, Senior Pastor

Peachtree Presbyterian identifies within its membership five LifeBands, or general groupings of persons experiencing similar life situations corresponding to age, marital status or another shared life experience, such as raising children. The LifeBands include young adults, families with children, families with students, adults and grand adults. Each LifeBand has a pastor assigned to oversee its specific needs and its

array of ministry opportunities. By addressing the specific challenges and needs experienced by people of different ages and at different life stages, the LifeBand format of ministry encourages the formation of relationships and community within the church.

Families with children and families with students form communities within the church. Peachtree baptized 180 babies in 2003, and the number of young families attending the church continues to grow. Peachtree meets the needs of this population with nationally accredited children's programs — both full- and half-day — during the week, as well as with innovative children's programs and dynamic student programs on Sunday mornings. Students have the opportunity to be involved in small groups during the week and in a teen-friendly worship setting on Sundays. Parents' needs are tended to as well, through small- and large-group Bible studies and a variety of family-oriented programming.

Every Sunday, members of all LifeBands and church guests can choose to attend one or more worship services. Choices include an intimate 30-minute worship service in Wilson Chapel, offering prayers, a meditation and communion; multiple traditional worship services with a sermon, hymns and reflective times of prayer, held in the sanctuary and led by the church's Chancel Choir and pastors; and a more contemporary service led by a worship team and band, which includes dynamic preaching, hymns and praise songs in a community atmosphere. All are welcome to a post-service lunch buffet in the church's Fellowship Hall. For those who cannot attend church in person, services are viewable live via Web cast from the church's Web site and are also televised locally. Additionally, the church holds structured discipleship opportunities including Sunday school and Bible studies for all ages.

Wednesdays at Peachtree bring a midweek opportunity for members to reaffirm and share their commitments to discipleship with other members of the Peachtree community. Adults and children can eat at the Fellowship Dinner, while adult singles can opt to dine with the Peachtree Supper Club if they so wish. Members can also participate in a variety of activities from Bible studies to choir practices.

Peachtree's wide array of musical opportunities includes numerous vocal choirs and hand bell choirs and currently involves more than 300 members, ages four and up. Men's and women's ministries, including a community-wide women's Bible study, meet weekly. The Prayer Ministry Team provides members with classes, resources and opportunities to grow in prayer. An assortment of small groups, retreats and special events is regularly organized through both LifeBand ministries and the groups described above.

Peachtree Presbyterian Church maintains an active involvement in numerous mission activities on both local and global scales. At 134 and counting, Peachtree has built more houses for Habitat for Humanity than any church in the world. Other Atlanta-area mission endeavors include Buckhead Christian Ministries, Atlanta Union Mission and the Salvation Army, among many others. On a global scale, in 2000, the church began a 10-year partnership with the Medical Benevolence Foundation, the China Christian Council and the Amity Foundation to help provide support for medical personnel, equipment, supplies and financial aid to a church-based hospital in China. The church carries the good news of Jesus Christ to the world through additional global outreach partnership programs in 15 countries (including Haiti, countries in the Middle East, Hungary, Russia and Brazil) on five continents.

Peachtree offers many other ministries designed to foster community. During times of personal crisis or pastoral emergencies, Peachtree's pastoral care resources offer support by fulfilling prayer requests, responding to questions about spirituality and providing counseling and support services through Peachtree Counseling Center. The Peachtree Presbyterian Gym and Fitness Center offers an array of cardio and strength training equipment, fitness classes, two full-sized courts for basketball and inline

Peachtree baptized 180 babies in 2003.

Peachtree's ministries include several nationally accredited children's programs.

skating, certified personal trainers with competitive rates, and a variety of specialty classes such as bridge, golf, Spanish and SAT prep, as well as many other learning and enrichment opportunities. The Peachtree Presbyterian Bookstore provides members with access to literary materials that can enhance their religious knowledge and education.

With its wide array of resources and the depth of its local and global mission involvement, Peachtree Presbyterian Church strives to honor and lift up the name of Jesus Christ. Peachtree Presbyterian Church aims to support its current and future members as they mature spiritually by encouraging them to worship regularly, grow intentionally and give of themselves generously through both stewardship and service in the name of Jesus Christ.

Transfiguration Catholic Church

To proclaim God the Father, Jesus the Savior, the Spirit the Life Giver and Healer, and all people as sisters and brothers, Transfiguration Catholic Church gathered in the banquet room of a local hotel and celebrated its first official Mass on November 13, 1977. Rooted in its initial 75 families who ventured on spiritual retreats twice a year, Transfiguration has continued this tradition, but now does so as a much larger, more prominent, formal and ardent religious community of northeast Cobb County.

For over a quarter century, the church has formed this enduring community by strengthening and nurturing relationships between its members, avidly upholding the Table of Word and Sacrament, living united in the rich Roman Catholic tradition, and serving as disciples and teachers. Monsignor Patrick Bishop and the Parochial Vicars preside over six Sunday Masses, one Saturday evening Mass and more than 60 different charitable, educational and spiritual ministries. With hundreds of volunteers and organizations that tenderly work with parishioners, Transfiguration is not only a religious organization spreading the Word of God, but a versatile source for those who seek comfort, knowledge and reflection.

On June 22, 1997, Transfiguration opened its new Parish Center to accommodate religious education classes, social functions, group meetings/activities and parish administration facilities. The people of Transfiguration use this Parish Center regularly to live out their faith through active ministries, such as child-care and preschool services, which are provided in the center's parish nursery, child-care site and preschool — all of which offer loving Christian care and development.

Transfiguration's Parish Religious Education Program (PREP) offers catechetical instruction based on the Catechism of the Catholic Church, the Scriptures and Church Tradition via Adult Education, ChrisTeen, and Preschool and Elementary Education Program (PEEP). The church's Adult Education program provides adults with ongoing opportunities to develop their faith, experience their surrounding community, and reflect on and increase their awareness of the presence of God. ChrisTeen is a comprehensive Youth Ministry Program for younger parishioners in the seventh through the 12th grades, involving catechetical instruction, retreats, recreational activities, worship, evangelization, justice, peace and service projects.

The church's Preschool and Elementary Education Program (PEEP) is designed to provide religious education including sacramental preparation programs and Vacation Bible School for children three years old through the sixth grade. For Spanish parishioners, Transfiguration also offers seminars for personal and spiritual growth and preparation for all the sacraments.

Transfiguration's Bringing Religious Instruction to Everyone (BRITE) program offers religious

Photos by Don Rank Photography

education classes to young persons from kindergarten to young adults with developmental disabilities. Its Rainbows program helps emotional children to cope with death, divorce, or any other painful transition. Additionally, its Order of Christian Initiation for Adults (OCIA) and Children (OCIC) programs provide the development needed for non-Catholics to become Catholic.

As an avid participant in community service, Transfiguration assists Marietta's Elizabeth Inn Shelter by making and serving meals to 65 people twice a month; is a partner with Habitat for Humanity, building and renovating houses at no profit for those in need; reinforces its view and understanding of the global Church by working with Haiti Ministry; and provides charitable assistance via its alliance with the St. Vincent de Paul Society.

In addition, Transfiguration benevolently supports AA; provides a space for individuals, couples and families to receive professional counseling on topics such as stress, worry, depression, relationships and addictions; promotes a Deaf Ministry to help the deaf fully participate in the faith life of the community of worship, social gatherings and educational opportunities; and offers grief support through its "Good Mourning" program, which provides one-on-one support for those who have lost a loved one.

In addition, Transfiguration's Health/Wellness Ministry provides education on health-related issues and assists with medical screenings; its Ministry of Caring visits the sick in their homes during their recovery period, taking communion to them in nursing homes, local hospitals and private homes; its church facilities support Narcotics Anonymous; its Respect for Life Ministries provide resources to promote respect for life "from womb to tomb" — providing services that do everything from helping individuals deal with unwanted pregnancies, to caring for the elderly and infirm; and its Wedding Guild Ministry aids parish couples through wedding preparation, including procedure, arrangement and rehearsal coordination.

Transfiguration Catholic Church sponsors Boy Scouts of America's Pack, Troop and Post 75. The church also sponsors the Girl Scouts of America's Daisies, Brownies, Girl Scouts and Juniors; the Knights of Columbus Council #10362; and Pax Christi, the national Catholic voice of 12,000 members that study and promote Christian nonviolence.

To facilitate communication and enjoyment among its Catholic community members, Transfiguration maintains a Friendship Circle, Men's Club, Newcomer's Wine and Cheese event, Social Committee, "Star of Heaven Quilters" club, variety of Support Groups, Baby-Sitting Co-op and CareerCare Ministry that provides spiritual and practical support to those in career transition.

Through its formal and non-formal religious servitude and many ministries, Transfiguration Catholic Church is an alive, vibrant and energetic community. Opening its arms to embrace all who wish to be a part of its family, Transfiguration considers itself a group of imperfect people struggling to be perfected in Christ. Not only will seekers find their spiritual needs satisfied, they will also encounter many smiling faces, a sincere openness to others, attentiveness to the Word of God and a deep sense of His presence.

Solvay Pharmaceuticals, Inc.

Solvay Pharmaceuticals is dedicated to helping people live the lives they desire. With this philosophy underpinning its efforts to discover, manufacture and market medically necessary products, the company leverages its unique scientific heritage and technical expertise from its U.S. headquarters in Marietta, Georgia, a suburb of Atlanta.

Over the years, the Solvay name has come to stand for scientific innovation, vision, and integrity. Today's Solvay Pharmaceuticals organization is rooted in its founding father's passion for progress.

In 1863, Belgian scientist and industrialist Ernest Solvay founded Solvay S.A., the parent company of Solvay Pharmaceuticals. Attesting to his highly regarded reputation in the scientific community, Ernest Solvay was also the renowned organizer of a landmark 1911 Council on Physics that assembled many of the day's leading scientists — including Einstein,

Planck, Curie, and Rutherford. As a result of his dedication to science, Ernest Solvay's scientific work and the company he formed paved the way for much pharmaceutical-related success.

Solvay Pharmaceuticals provides relief to millions of people affected by conditions in the therapeutic areas of cardiology, gastroenterology, mental health, and women's health. In recent years, Solvay Pharmaceuticals has expanded its breadth by acquiring a cluster of specialty products that fulfill specific, unmet medical needs. Among the company's products are first-of-their-kind treatments and medications ranked No.1 in their categories. Solvay Pharmaceuticals' product portfolio continues to focus on helping people live the lives they desire.

Always seeking new ways to help patients, Solvay Pharmaceuticals works closely with its global network of R&D colleagues to develop solutions for patients' medical needs. The company is perpetually engaged in the process of developing and testing new treatment options in its selected therapeutic areas. Solvay Pharmaceuticals' human

health care strategy emphasizes growth through the discovery, development, licensing, and acquisition of pharmaceuticals and technologies that complement its therapeutic categories. The company also pursues alliances that meet both its aggressive sales objectives and the needs of its partners.

Solvay Pharmaceuticals proudly continues its tradition of bringing innovative medical therapies to market. A prime example is CREON®, the first pancreatic extract to be prescribed for symptoms associated with Cystic Fibrosis in 1900 and still marketed today in the United States as CREON® MINIMICROS-PHERES®. More recently, Solvay Pharmaceuticals and its wholly owned subsidiary, Unimed Pharmaceuticals, launched AndroGel®, the first topical testosterone gel approved to treat men with low levels of this important hormone. Another of Solvay Pharmaceuticals' unique offerings is MARINOL®; the only approved form of the key active ingredient in marijuana, MARINOL® is an appetite stimulant for AIDS patients and an antiemetic to stem the nausea and vomiting associated with cancer chemotherapy.

As a company that cares for people, Solvay Pharmaceuticals channels its financial and human resources toward improving the health and well-being of people in the communities where its employees live and work. Solvay Pharmaceuticals' designated outreach areas — health (mental and physical), youth and older adults — align with its corporate goals while enriching employees and their families through volunteer opportunities.

The company pursues working relationships with organizations in communities such as Marietta, Georgia; Baudette, Minnesota — the site of its manufacturing facility; and cities around the country where its sales professionals are based.

Whether manufacturing and marketing medically necessary products or creating strong links with local communities, Solvay Pharmaceuticals remains committed to helping people live the lives they desire.

Southside Medical Center

Southside Medical Center is one of America's oldest community-based health care centers. Located in southeast Atlanta, its primary mission is to deliver health care services to Atlanta's poor and working poor.

The center was established in 1967 to address the overcrowding, long wait-times and inconvenient location of the local hospital. These barriers caused many to avoid seeking treatment, which exasperated their condition and drove up the cost of their health care.

Community and business leaders along with federal health officials responded to this crisis by creating the health center, designed to provide affordable and accessible family-oriented medical services.

For 36 years, the facility operated out of a 100-year-old renovated mattress factory and worked with schools, other health care facilities, and community and human service organizations to develop programs that increased access to high-quality health care.

Southside Medical Center quickly established a reputation as one of Georgia's premiere providers of comprehensive primary care. Patients gained access to internal medicine, obstetrics, gynecology, pediatrics, dentistry and optometry. As the need arose, Southside added specialty services in urology, cardiology, podiatry, and chiropractic, to name a few. Laboratory, pharmacy, and radiology services also became available, as well as free and convenient transportation services.

But Southside did not stop there. As years progressed, satellite clinics in Cobb, Clayton, Dekalb, and Gwinnett counties were added in response to the demand for service locations beyond southeast Atlanta. Several of these clinics offer services primarily in Spanish to cater to the growing Hispanic population.

Despite its already extensive services, the center continues to develop programs that will help overcome barriers and provide quality care to a diverse population.

In 1999, Southside Medical Center was among the first community health centers in Georgia to meet the accreditation standards of the Joint Commission on Accreditation of Health Care Organizations (JCAHO) and has since been recognized by the National Association of Community Health Centers as one of the best primary health care delivery systems in the country for the medically underserved.

The center moved into a new three-story, 46,200-square-foot facility in 2003 across the street from the old facility, resulting in a surge in utilization of much needed services. In the first year of the move, Southside Medical Center saw a surge of over 10 percent in client visits and has the capacity to see over 300,000 visits annually.

For many years, Southside Medical Center has been the largest of its kind in Georgia and has ranked among the 10 largest community health care centers in the country. Its original goal of bringing highly trained physicians and important medical services into Atlanta's inner-city neighborhoods is being accomplished every day, with compassion, dedication and excellence.

Dr. David Williams, a family practitioner with a public health and administrative background, has been an integral part of this organization's growth for over 13 years. He assumed leadership in 1998, and since then, has moved the organization into the 21st century with innovative ideas on how to serve the community and by spearheading the construction of a new, $8 million facility.

Southside Medical Center is poised to play a vital role in the health of the metropolitan community.

Solarcom® Independent Technology Solutions®

Gone are the days of three-part memos and fax machines. Today's fast-paced world of e-Business, the Web and digital communication has created demand for robust information technology (IT) infrastructures and the need to protect sensitive data that is more valuable than the equipment on which it sits.

Solarcom® is an independent technology consultant and solution provider that helps companies solve real business problems such as increasing competitive advantage and sales, reducing costs or improving productivity. Since 1976, the Atlanta-based IT expert has steadily grown and evolved as the dynamic field of technology has advanced and changed the way business is conducted.

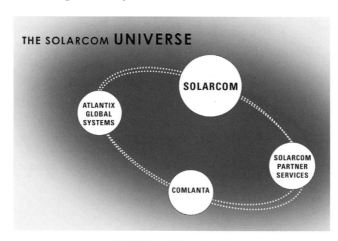

THE SOLARCOM **UNIVERSE**

Quick Facts

- Established in 1976
- Largest independent technology solution provider in Georgia
- Approximately $400 million revenue and growing
- Approximately 300 Employees
- Thousands of loyal customers
- Headquartered in Atlanta, GA, with 30+ locations
- Approximately 140,000+ square-foot campus/ 14,000+square-foot integration center/ 36,000+square-foot warehouse
- Approximately 40 engineers
- Continuously recognized for record growth by:
  - VARBusiness 500
  - Gwinnett County's List of Top Privately Held Companies
  - *Atlanta Business Chronicle's* List of Top High-Technology Companies

The Solarcom family of companies (Solarcom LLC, Atlantix Global Systems® LLC, Comlanta® LLC and Solarcom Partner Services℠) has the experience businesses need to evaluate, design and implement technology solutions while making sure they see a true return on investment. As a result, companies can focus efforts on their core business, secure in knowing they have partnered for the best in technology expertise with Solarcom.

A MESSAGE FROM CHAIRMAN AND CEO I. ERIC PROCKOW

One of the traits that differentiates Solarcom from its competitors and other large companies is the unique culture of caring that has been fostered over the years. It is rare to have employees stay with a company 15 or 20+ years, yet it is commonplace at Solarcom.

That spirit of true concern for employees and customers alike starts with the executive team and helps make Solarcom a special place to come to work.

Employees enjoy personal touches such as:
- Service Appreciation Week
- Employee of the Quarter Awards
- Co-Employee Recognition Awards
- Quota Club trips to first-class resorts in exotic locales
- Annual events including Family Picnic, Holiday Luncheon and Holiday Party
- Tickets to the Solarcom suite at Philips Arena

Year after year, activities such as these strengthen Solarcom's sense of family and help say, "thank you for your efforts and a job well done."

Customers, too, are valued and receive an absolute commitment to making sure issues are handled to their satisfaction. Solarcom engages in long-term strategic business relationships with its clients that are solution-oriented, not transaction-based. Customers gain access to:
- Campus tours
- Technical laboratories
- Executive Briefing Center meetings
- Educational seminars on a wide range of topics
- Engineering expertise
- Extensive partner networking

The same sense of caring and dedication manifests itself to the greater Atlanta community in various ways as Solarcom continues to offer its support through efforts such as:
- Sponsorship of the Atlanta Thrashers® and its charitable projects
- Sponsorship of the Metro Atlanta Police/Fire hockey team and the Atlanta Burn Foundation
- Sponsorship of the Promina® Corporate Run/Walk
- Sponsorship of the Make-A-Wish Foundation®
- Donations to the annual Norcross Cooperative Ministry Holiday Toy Drive
- Donations to and participation in American Red Cross® blood drives

Finally, Solarcom is dedicated to upholding the highest standards in business and has built the company around such values as:
- **Commitment**: dedication to each other and to customers
- **Quality**: attention to detail and excellence
- **Service**: thoughtful concern and commitment to act
- **Leadership**: responsible influence with accountability
- **Integrity**: assertion to do what is right
- **Vision**: insight and forward-thinking expertise

Thanks to the people who take the time to make a difference, Solarcom is a quality force in the technology industry and at the same time, maintains a warm and friendly demeanor.

A HISTORY OF SUCCESS

Since 1976 Solarcom has grown and evolved its IT-infrastructure focus in a strategic and deliberate manner, keeping customers ahead of the technology curve.

In the 1970s when it was known as Sun Data, the corporation was a leader in the IBM® secondary market. As technology shifted away from mainframes, so did the company, focusing efforts on the upgrade, configuration and leasing of pre-owned midrange computers.

In 1985 a disaster recovery group was formed in response to the demand of midrange system users for a flexible yet affordable form of back-up assistance.

In 1988 IBM introduced the AS/400® and for a period the corporation became one of the largest resellers of midrange products in the United States, building an entire support organization including training, software support, distribution, conversion and communication.

Solarcom is a proud sponsor of the Atlanta Thrashers® hockey team.

An emphasis on values like Commitment, Quality, Service, Leadership, Integrity and Vision sets Solarcom apart.

The business focus further evolved in the 1990s — concentrating on infrastructure solutions with best-of-breed technology partners and the establishment of a more formal Professional Services team. Expertise grew in Internetworking, UNIX® and Windows®-related products. The company also developed partnerships with Cisco Systems®, EMC®, Sun Microsystems®, Hewlett-Packard®, VERITAS™, IBM®, Microsoft® and other organizations as part of its growth strategy. In fact, Solarcom still stands alone as the only independent provider among Cisco Systems Gold Certified channel partners.

SOLARCOM TODAY-A UNIVERSE OF SOLUTIONS

After more than 20 years in business, in 1999 Sun Data changed its name to Solarcom. The new name is a

reflection of an expanding reach to more than just the traditional IT data center.

Together, the Solarcom family of companies presents a comprehensive resource for IT infrastructure and financial solutions that is unmatched in the industry.

SOLARCOM®, LLC
Independent IT Consulting and Integration

Solarcom's services provide:

- Internetworking; robust network infrastructures connecting employees and offices to one another
- Enterprise Systems; server consolidation and clustering to ease management, increase scalability, application performance and high availability
- Storage; networked storage infrastructure, data and information lifecycle management
- Telecommunications; contract analysis and management, billing audits and voice/data telecom services

Solarcom offers integrated infrastructure solutions designed by expert engineers and consultants whose product, market and industry knowledge is unmatched. And because Solarcom represents multiple vendors, customers gain a consultative ally and the ability to leverage Solarcom's Independent Advantage™.

Financial Solutions

Today, Information Technology projects require measurable results to even be considered for approval. Solarcom understands the business requirements of IT and can measure Total Cost of Ownership (TCO) as well as provide financial services products that help customers:

- Qualify for off-balance sheet financing to improve financial ratios
- Maximize tax benefits

- Achieve price/performance efficiencies by matching expenses to benefits and paying for technology only when it is deployed and utilized

With Solarcom financial solutions, customers can control and reduce IT costs, eliminate surprises, make budgets predictable and realize significant savings to the bottom line.

ATLANTIX GLOBAL SYSTEMS®, LLC
The Hardware Experts

One of the world's largest brokers of secondary market IT hardware, Atlantix enables customers to achieve significant cost savings through the purchase, sale, lease, rental, or consignment of equipment.

Atlantix's multilingual technology consultants serve the global market in more than 80 countries, speak over 15 languages and work around-the-clock to accommodate all time zones. With over 3,000 sources for equipment around the world, Atlantix has consistent access to the latest technology and hardware, so if a piece of equipment is not in inventory, it can usually be obtained within 24-48 hours.

A 36,000-square-foot warehouse provides Atlantix with the ability to procure necessary equipment ahead of project schedules and hold it for delivery or to stage it through an on-site integration center, leveraging the expertise of approximately 40 engineers.

All purchases are entered in a real-time order tracking system and radio frequency scanners keep track of every step to ensure that orders are shipped complete and on-time. Shipping progress can then be monitored from anywhere in the world using a web-based interface.

Finally, all Atlantix equipment is guaranteed eligible for manufacturer's maintenance and can often be re-certified by the manufacturer on-site prior to shipment.

SOLARCOM PARTNER SERVICES℠ (SPS)
Telecom Lifecycle Management

SPS provides:
- Telecom consulting
- Telecom audit and recovery services
- Telecom services as a Master Reseller for AT&T®, Qwest®, MCI® and others
- Provisioning management and integration
- Agent/Reseller access to solutions from the Solarcom family of companies

Carrier services and telecommunications-related expenses are among a company's largest IT expenditures, yet more than 50 percent of large enterprises don't have accurate disclosure and centralized control of these costs. According to analysts, on average 7-12 percent of an organization's telecom expenditures are in error.

Solarcom Partner Services is a national telecommunications consultant and provider of carrier services. SPS offers customers help in catching billing errors, renegotiating contracts and leveraging its size in dealing with the large national telecom companies to help simplify a problem that is unmanaged in most businesses.

Moreover, Solarcom Partner Services can bring the breadth and depth of solutions offered by the entire Solarcom family of companies to Agents and Reseller partners without a significant investment of additional time or capital.

COMLANTA®, LLC
Cost-Effective Disaster Recovery

Comlanta provides services such as:
- Disaster recovery
- Remote backup and replication
- Focused hosting or co-location of equipment

Business information is as vulnerable as it is valuable and can be susceptible to a wide variety of consequence. From the largest forces of nature to terrorism, hackers, malicious viruses and worms, or even simply a cup of coffee spilled on a server, there is a need for business recovery services.

Half the companies that lose their data in a disaster never open their doors again. To ensure a customer's future in the face of the unexpected, Comlanta offers a wide range of reliable, scalable and secure business recovery solutions as well as Disaster Recovery (D/R) planning and consulting services. As Sun Data, the company pioneered midrange data recovery in the mid-1980s, and today offers comprehensive Business Recovery options that range from facility recovery space to dedicated, redundant system architecture.

In the event of a problem, customers may rest assured they are covered and have the insurance of a reliable, secure off-site data center from which they can run their business and retrieve their valuable data. And because of all the resources the Solarcom family of companies has access to, Comlanta business recovery solutions are delivered at the highest level of service and at an affordable price.

A BRIGHT FUTURE

Much like its corporate logo of escalating suns, Solarcom has risen to the forefront of IT consulting and continues to establish value in ever-larger accounts. As a company who embraces its history, values its people and continues to build on a solid foundation, Solarcom is well positioned to capitalize on its successes and explore an ever-widening horizon that holds a very bright future indeed.

With brick-and-mortar investments like a 36,000-square-foot warehouse, Solarcom is able to help customers with the logistics of large IT projects.

Since 1976, Solarcom has served over 8,000 clients with its team of IT professionals.

Definition 6

Michael Kogon has watched the Internet and its related technology grow from being a novelty for businesses in 1994 to being an essential part of today's commercial climate.

"We've gone from an attitude of, 'I'll try it,' to 'It would be nice to have,' to 'It's the way to do business,'" Kogon says. "I don't know of any successful business today that hasn't incorporated the Internet into its operations."

Not by coincidence, Definition 6, the Atlanta-based integrated marketing and technology firm that Kogon co-founded in 1997, has grown along with the popularity of Internet technology, at a rate of about 20 percent a year.

Kogon, who has a background in business management and advertising, is the chief executive officer of the 50-employee firm. Co-founder Jordan Fladell is its chief sales officer.

> **Definition 6 offers its clients technological expertise ranging from strengthening internal communications to designing sales-generating and award-winning Web sites.**

Definition 6 offers its clients technological expertise ranging from strengthening internal communications to designing sales-generating and award-winning Web sites. Integrated marketing has been one of the company's most powerful services in helping marketing and IT departments succeed.

Using top technology and business experts, Definition 6 helps clients find solutions to real-world scenarios. Its specialties include Strategy; Internet-Based Business Systems; Information Architecture; Interactive Marketing; Customer Relationship Management; Hosting; and much more.

Definition 6 has created a one-stop shop for clients who are seeking both marketing and Web-based services. It offers fully integrated marketing campaigns, including online, offline and print production services. The approach has brought the company steady growth.

"We started our company during an exciting time in the Internet/technology marketplace, and survived in a most difficult period as well, so it's quite an achievement to still be in business today," Kogon says. "So many other companies fail to reach this point — only one in 10 new companies survive their first five years in business — so we are very pleased that Definition 6 has continued to expand and mature with each passing year."

Fladell offers insight into the reasons for the company's growth.

"We have continued to survive, even as so many other Internet consulting companies closed down when the economy suddenly turned downward in 2001," Fladell says. "We do great work here, but our accomplishments in the industry always tie back to our belief in traditional business common sense."

Definition 6 has emerged as a leader in Atlanta's business community by bringing marketing and technology together to help clients prosper.

"We realize that while marketing and technology go hand in hand, marketing and IT professionals may often not speak the same language," Kogon says. "We serve as a translator and consultant, helping both teams understand that they face many of the same challenges and can create efficiencies by working together. Ultimately, our efforts culminate in increased revenues and lower costs for our clients."

The company's founding philosophy is to deliver effective, bottom-line results, one customer at a time. The philosophy accounts for successes with clients including Beazer Homes, Novartis Ophthalmic, Supervalu, Georgia Pacific, Southern Company, AFC and many others.

When Beazer Homes became a client of Definition 6, the Atlanta-based company was the 19th-largest homebuilder in the nation; Kogon says, "Five years later it was the sixth largest." For Beazer, Definition 6 developed a Web site that helped the company sell more than 100 homes online, and the number of annual visitors to the site increased from 250,000 to 3.3 million in five years. Beazer's site also won the 2003 Gold Medal Award from the National Association of Homebuilders. Builders have become one of the categories of specialization for Definition 6.

For Novartis, a Swiss pharmaceutical company, Definition 6 developed a Web site to promote the company's anti-allergy eye drop, Zaditor. Over 100,000 users registered and it was selected as the best Web site by the eHealth Care Council. Novartis uses the Internet to communicate with doctors and its sales force, as well as consumers, Kogon says.

For Atlanta-based Georgia Pacific — the manufacturer of products including Brawny, Quilted Northern and Dixie Cups — Definition 6 developed a Web site to allow the company to communicate better with customers. The site, allyourrooms.com, offers lifestyle tips and product promotions. The combination of classic marketing techniques with Internet technology has been "highly successful," Kogon says.

As impressive as the growth of Internet technology and Definition 6 has been to this point, Kogon predicts more impressive growth in the future. "I see us on the verge of making the Internet an equal partner with all other forms of communication," he says. "Already, just about 100 percent of goods are available on the Internet, even though the Internet never will make up 100 percent of sales. Even catalog companies took some orders by phone."

The Internet offers many advantages that account for its continued growth and popularity. "It's so easy to just pick up a mouse and figure out how to do something, compared to using a manual," Kogon says. "And with the Internet, two or more people can communicate instantly and at no cost.

Not only is Internet technology advanced, it is dependable. "The technology itself was designed to survive catastrophe, and we live in a more and more uncertain world," Kogon says. "It is the technology for an ever-evolving world — and I still feel like we're in the early days."

As of 2003, 64 percent of Americans were online and the number was growing at a rate of 20 percent per year. "The next wave in the Internet will be wireless," Kogon says. "I see us remaining in the forefront."

Michael Kogon, chief executive officer of Definition 6

As much as Internet technology may advance and change, one thing will stay the same, Kogon and Fladell say: Definition 6 will remain based in Atlanta.

"We consciously decided to make and retain Atlanta as our headquarters," Kogon says. "The city has a well-educated work force, a pro-business government and it is re-energizing its infrastructure. We're also very involved in community and civic groups."

Scientific Games

LOTTERIES: HISTORICAL ROOTS RUN CENTURIES DEEP

Lotteries and good causes... they go together like fun and excitement.

As far back as history can go, lotteries have helped shape the world's political, social and cultural landscape. For centuries, lotteries have served as a crucial instrument of public policy, and the now-thriving global industry continues to supply revenue to a multitude of beneficiary programs, many that would not be possible without lottery funding.

Take Keno, which today is enjoyed by Georgians in adult social establishments throughout the state. This popular numbers game is believed to have been invented in China, a full century B.C., to raise money for armies. Similar examples abound on virtually every continent, in virtually every century, and are far too numerous to list here.

Lotteries were also the mainstay of growth in the colonial days. As early as 1612, a lottery was operated to finance the first American colony at Jamestown. Many of the original 13 states operated lotteries, and, just as

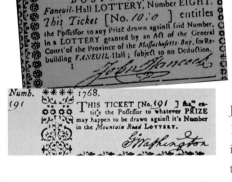

government leaders do today, American colonists used the proceeds for schools, roads, bridges, even churches.

George Washington operated a lottery in 1768 to finance construction of the Mountain Road designed to open the way west from Virginia. John Hancock operated a lottery in 1767 for rebuilding historic Faneuil Hall in Boston. Lottery proceeds in early times also helped to build and support colleges such as Harvard, Yale and Princeton.

Thomas Jefferson perhaps said it best, hailing the lottery as "the perfect tax, laid only upon the willing."

Most Georgians would be surprised to learn that the Georgia Lottery is only one of 214 government-authorized lotteries in the world. In 2003 worldwide lottery sales topped $130 billion. Safely assume that 30 percent of that figure, or $39 billion, went to lottery beneficiary programs and very quickly one gets the sense of just how much good lotteries are doing all over the world, including right here in Georgia with the popular HOPE Scholarship and Pre-Kindergarten programs.

Today lotteries are possible in the United States only when specifically authorized by state law. The first state to authorize a lottery in what has been labeled "the modern-day era" was New Hampshire in 1964. In a November 1992 referendum, Georgians gave then-Governor Zell Miller authorization to start the Georgia Lottery, which he did in 1993. In 2004 Tennessee and North Dakota became the newest U.S. states to start a lottery, and Oklahoma authorized a lottery in late 2004. Not including Oklahoma, there are 41 U.S. lotteries, and aggregate annual U.S.lottery sales exceed $45 billion.

SCIENTIFIC GAMES: WELCOME TO OUR WORLD

As is evident by the numbers, the lottery industry is big business with a global reach; thus, world-class technology plays a critical role in the industry's enduring success and in helping lotteries maintain public trust.

Few people outside the lottery industry know this, but printing lottery tickets, and keeping them secure, is far more complicated than printing currency. Lottery tickets pass through 18 to 21 different printing stations on custom-built presses, each almost the length of a football field. Sophisticated computer programs communicate with state-of-the-art ink-jet imagers, which print the winning and losing numbers, play symbols and validation codes — all onto an area of the ticket the size of a matchbook, at press speeds of up to 1,000 feet per minute. Unique bar codes are also simultaneously printed on the back of each ticket. And should one of the inkjets ever clog, suddenly and without notice, that losing "1" can appear to the player to be a winning "7."

In short, there's simply no margin for error. Every day is a high-stakes, high-wire act.

Welcome to the world of Scientific Games, the Alpharetta, Georgia-based high-tech company that produces more instant scratch-off tickets for more lotteries than all other companies combined — nearly 15 billion annually. That's B...as in billion! And that output speaks only for the printed products group, which includes computer programmers, digital graphic artists, web press operators, quality assurance technicians and customer account representatives.

There's also the systems group. Mention these gifted individuals and one begins speaking a slightly different language: the language of giant jackpots and intense pressure. Stop for a moment to consider just how reliable products have to be when — on any given Tuesday, Wednesday, Friday or Saturday — lotteries may be offering millions of eager consumers a $300 million jackpot. Imagine the clerk behind the counter, looking out at the crush of jackpot-day players and having to rely on a single lottery terminal and central system to print and record, in the blink of an eye, hundreds, perhaps thousands, of tickets purchased in the waning moments leading up to the drawing.

Imagine having to tell the lottery, within seconds after the drawing, if anyone won the Mega Millions or Powerball jackpot, how many had won, at which retail outlets, which cities and which states.

Does all this suggest that lotto machines and transaction processing systems need to be mission-critical and the best-of-breed technologically? You'd better believe it. And the group behind these products had better be sophisticated and knowledgeable as well.

SCIENTIFIC GAMES: A GLOBAL TECHNOLOGY LEADER

Scientific Games is a global technology leader and the world's second-largest provider of lottery products, systems and services. It is the largest division of New York-based Scientific Games Corporation, which, through its Scientific Games Racing division, also holds a dominant market position in pari-mutuel gaming.

Think Belmont Stakes. Think satellite feeds of live horse racing to hundreds of off-track betting facilities. Think immediate redemption of millions of winning horse racing and jai alai tickets every single day at tracks all over the world and one begins to understand the exciting world of Scientific Games Racing.

Today Scientific Games Corporation is a fast-growing, publicly-traded gaming company (NASDAQ: SGMS),

employing more than 3,200 people in strategic, customer-centric locations worldwide. Yet the organization's heart and soul resides in the Alpharetta technology and manufacturing center, where over 850 of the 3,200+ are employed.

Over the past year, Scientific Games Corporation began integrating its racing systems and other groups from out-of-state in with the lottery systems and printed product groups already in Alpharetta. The addition of these high-tech, highly educated individuals further cements Scientific Games' standing as the second largest employer in Forsyth County, Georgia.

Scientific Games has been a Georgia company since 1974. Over the past 30 years, steady, robust growth has necessitated relocation within Atlanta on four separate occasions; the last move brought the company to its current Alpharetta address in 1992. Since then, Scientific Games has expanded its Alpharetta operation four times, including a $15 million, 90,000 square-foot expansion completed December 2004. The full facility is now 340,000 square feet.

From Arizona to Zimbabwe, including all points in between and beyond, lotteries and racetracks place their confidence in Scientific Games people, products and performance.

Scientific Games... Winning The World Over.

Hewlett-Packard Company

In 1939 no one could have known that the company that young engineers Bill Hewlett and David Packard were starting in a Palo Alto, California, garage with $538 and a handful of good ideas would grow to be one of the largest and most innovative technology companies in the world. But it has.

Pushing technology toward the 21st century is something that Hewlett-Packard (HP) has been doing since its earliest days. Throughout its history, innovation has been a part of the culture of HP. That innovation has brought the world a myriad of products that have helped change the way people live and do business.

From its first product in the 1940s — the resistance-capacitance audio oscillator, an electronic instrument used to test sound equipment — to the Tablet PC, the DVD Moviewriter and other technologies that have come about with the start of the new century, HP's hallmark has been to push back the frontiers of technology and move the world forward, both in the boardroom and in the living room.

David Packard (left) and Bill Hewlett developed an innovative audio oscillator in this Palo Alto, California, garage in 1939. From these humble beginnings has grown one of the world's largest and most innovative technology companies.

HP's Atlanta Business Center

In November 1957, after 18 years as a privately held company, HP sold its first stock and became publicly traded. Little more than a year later it opened its first manufacturing plant outside of the United States in Boblingen, West Germany.

In the time since then HP has grown to serve more than one billion customers across 170 countries and is a leading global provider of products, technologies, solutions and services to consumers and businesses. HP has had a presence in Atlanta since 1962.

HP's $4 billion annual investment in research and development fuels the invention of new generations of products, solutions and technologies to better serve customers and enter new markets. Today the company's offerings span IT infrastructure, personal computing and access devices, global services, and imaging and printing.

While the scale and reach of HP's business has changed over its history, its commitment to the communities in which it does business hasn't. Besides being known for its technology and innovation, HP has also become known as a good corporate citizen. From its earliest days HP has given back to communities through contributions of money, equipment and time. The value of the generosity of HP and its employees reaches well into the millions of dollars each year.

Making lives better, whether through cutting-edge technology or through a tradition of caring and involvement, is what sets HP apart.

Partners & Web Site index